T0208955

VIBRATIONAL ALIGNMENT

A Guide to Understanding
Who You Are and Why You Are Here

SARAH MEGAN SPENCER, MSN, FNP

BALBOA.PRESS
A DIVISION OF HAY HOUSE

Balboa Press books may be ordered through booksellers or by contacting:

Balboa Press
A Division of Hay House
1663 Liberty Drive
Bloomington, IN 47403
www.balboapress.com
1 (877) 407-4847

Scripture quotations marked NIV are taken from The Holy Bible, New International Version®, NIV® Copyright © 1973, 1978, 1984, 2011 by Biblica, Inc.® Used by permission. All rights reserved worldwide.

Print information available on the last page.

ISBN: 978-1-9822-3913-8 (sc)
ISBN: 978-1-9822-3915-2 (hc)
ISBN: 978-1-9822-3914-5 (e)

Library of Congress Control Number: 2019919365

Balboa Press rev. date: 12/12/2019

CONTENTS

PART I: UNDERSTANDING VIBRATION

PART II: VIBRATIONAL ALIGNMENT MASTERY

DEDICATION

To:

All the unchanging, ever-changing cooperative components of my life that guide me along the way back to my source.

My first taste of unconditional love, Gage. You breathe life into my world just by being you.

My second love, Blake. You captivated my attention and led me to freedom through your daily pursuit for greatness … by following your bliss.

My third love, Beau. You teach me balance and how to be authentic, genuine, thoughtful, and just go with the flow.

My latest love, best friend and mirror…Mike.

Thank you, my fascinating, masculine counterparts for the gift of your existence.

INTRODUCTION

Congratulations. You are here with me, and it is no coincidence that you are. As I type this, I hold the intention that what you are about to read is undeniably written just for you. I know you have been at the same crossroads as I have encountered, and this book will guide you as you embark on the next part of your journey. I am a seeker, and so are you. Isn't it amazing to know that there is a universal delivery system just waiting to offer the seeker a guided understanding in the exact way that we need at the exact time that we need it? I have encountered the age-old dilemma of "What is my purpose?" and "What are we doing here?" my whole life. This book is the condensed, written version of my cooperative components and the leading-edge understanding of humanity's life purpose from my point of attraction. This book will offer leading-edge thoughts and a collection of reproducible processes identified by my life experience as well as leading-edge thinkers along the way.

My personal and professional history have provided me the unique ability to connect the dots on a large-scale perspective. My childhood provided my focused attention to detail, with minimal interference from peer opinion and perspective. This enhanced my ability to fine-tune my internal intuition or sixth sense. My teenage years led me into a backward-forward motion, providing me with inspiration and motivation to evolve into the masterpiece that made its appearance so many years ago on a hot July night. This life experience is nothing short of a master puzzle challenging the brave to stretch out of the cookie-cutter skin shells into unique contributing masterpieces.

Once my daily inspiration arrived in 1997, life would never be the same. The following twenty years consisted of undergraduate and graduate school studies surrounding human experience and the care of afflicted individuals. I obtained an associate degree in nursing, followed by a bachelor's degree in nursing, while raising two lively boys. Immediately following my undergraduate college graduation, my third son propelled my desire to pursue graduate school training along with work experience and mom-life credentialing. Upon conclusion of graduate school and receiving a master's degree of science in nursing, I became a certified family nurse practitioner.

I account my authority in the self-development world to the previously mentioned cooperative components and the following years of clinical training and experience with chronically ill and terminally ill patients. From 2005 to 2018, I acquired the most exquisite experiences and understanding from the many patients who were divinely placed upon my path. I truly felt that I was the one receiving a gift with each encounter. From 1997 to the current day, I have received and continue to receive inspiration and fine-tuning to conscious awareness from my three sons, my siblings, and many generational beings who have graced my path. All have left lasting impressions, improved my awareness, and expanded my consciousness.

Lastly, I recognize the powerful thought leaders who helped provide the basis for the alignment and understanding that inspired the evolution of the character living and writing this book. The divine timing of Andy Shaw and *A Bug Free Mind*. The Rapid Planning Method process of the official freak of nature and divine being Tony Robbins. Esther, Jerry, and Abraham Hicks for the culmination and collective understanding of vibrational alignment from Esther's point of attraction. Danielle LaPorte and the pure genius of Core Desired Feelings and her beautifully illustrated and designed planners. The Spirit Junkie, Gabby Bernstein. The Why man, Simon Sinek. The vulnerable-courageous Brene Brown. The beautiful, authentic soul of Mastin Kipp. Don Miguel Ruiz and the *Four Agreements*, which changed the direction of my life. Author and kick-ass human Mel Robbins. Robin Sharma and his consistent, world-class outpouring of pure divine intelligence. The authenticity and courage of the leader and high performer Brendon Burchard. David Engleman. *The Wayne Dyer*. The one and only Jason Silva, who lives his art through the emotions of passion and appreciation. The powerful forces of Neville Goddard, Jack Kornfield, Gary Zukav, David R. Hawkins, Marianne Williamson—the president of political love☺, Byron Katie, Gabor Maté, Gary V, Gay Hendricks, Steven Kotler and Jaime Wheal—the Flow guys, Genevieve Davis, Vishen Lakhiani and his massive contribution—Mindvalley, Deepak Chopra, Rachel Hollis, Dale Carnegie, Ryan Holiday, Eckhart Tolle, and the Kosmic Ken Wilber. The voice and intelligence of YouTube, which has delivered

Jim Rohn, John Maxwell, Bob Proctor, Marisa Peer, Dr. Bruce Lipton, Oprah, and my current audio and online addiction Dr. Joe Dispenza, whose book *Becoming Supernatural* provided another, maybe the greatest, synchronicity to the internal validation of my experience and understanding. Lastly, the aspiration and gift of Tom Bilyeu and *Impact Theory*, through edgy conversations with visionaries about things that actually matter. I can't wait to meet and experience every one of these divine manifestations, although we have met many, many times in the comfort of my personal home, car, and internal mind laboratory.

In conclusion, I have done my homework. I have lived through emotional tragedy. I have experienced neural connections on a kosmic highway and connected the dots. I have educated myself within the dualistic world of university, self-development, and clinical experience. My hobbies include a fondness of quantum physics, the Audible app, and "Cam University", and mediocre socializing skills with no interest in raising the bar in that arena, other than with the visionaries of the world. I have physically experienced significant quantum leaps, a variety of contrast, and the collective desire for change. My personal vibration has fluctuated from passion to needy to depressed to contentment to appreciation and pure love. My desire is to focus my daily attention on my personal alignment with source and then ripple the appreciation for life and love to all who cross my vibrational path. I am the collective manifestation known as the Vibrational Snob.

PART I

UNDERSTANDING VIBRATION

CHAPTER 1

THE BASICS

Let me take you to a flat little piece of land in West Virginia, surrounded by overgrown weeds and brush on the right side of a quaint little white house. If you stood on your tiptoes, you could barely grab hold of clusters of small, fragrant white flowers on the vine. Standing close by on a breezy day, you would feel engulfed by the sweet, floral scent. One deep breath was not enough. I would hold a cluster in my left hand while pinching the base of the flower with my right thumb and pointer finger, gently tugging till it popped off just a little. I slid out the long core to reveal one itty-bitty drop of sweetness and carefully touched it to my tongue. I smiled. But the enjoyment of the sweetness was only part of what attracted me.

I realize now that the playful, inquisitive little girl was manifested pure positive energy. She arrived just in time to shake things up a bit.

This little girl woke up every day looking for the new and the exciting. She answered almost every comment with *why*—not out of rebellion, but out of a pure desire to understand. She wanted to see and file away everything she could. She was a seeker. She had medium-length, coarse brown hair and scattered freckles on her nose and cheeks. She wore whatever was on her bed or on the floor— never concerned with herself but only this gigantic world she woke up to every day. I have few memories of my younger years, but the few I do have are as vivid as if they happened yesterday.

You most likely remember your little self. Inquisitive. Happy. Playful. Full of life. Watching life to absorb all that you could as if it were a documentary in front of your eyes. I did not know that I was processing every detail, but I was: The honeysuckle and its sweet smell. The breeze. The honey. Inhalation. Exhalation. My brother. The little white house. These are some of the first cooperative components that I remember. All were necessary. All were provided just for me, at just the right time and in just the right place. Perfection.

We all manifest in this world with an inner guidance—a GPS system, if you will. The problem is that we are not taught to identify or understand it precisely. In fact, we are guided off course by nearly every living, breathing human we cross paths with. However, our dogs have it right!

Imagine that you wake up each morning and know exactly what to do to make your day the best day of your life. Understanding who you are and why you are here will give you the tools to live your best life every day. This book was not written to teach you something new; it is a guide to help you remember what you already know or have experienced. It will help you understand who you are, why you are here, and how you can consciously guide your life to create whatever you desire. I will share many of my experiences and understandings of life, as well as the pattern of understanding that I received over the course of my life. I believe my gift to the world is my unique contribution, my collection of cooperative components, and my understanding of alignment.

By seeking my purpose, I found my purpose. In finding my purpose, I found alignment. I was always seeking alignment. You were always seeking alignment. We simply did not realize that we were looking for alignment. We thought we were looking for happiness and success. Ultimately, success and happiness are what all people seek. From the perspective of an unconscious mind, we arrive here on this planet and from that point experience life from our own personal viewpoint. We are born and raised by individuals divinely placed for the evolution of our highest and best experience.

"You do not know my past," you might say. "I was abused and rejected and treated very unfairly my whole life." True, I do not know you personally, but here is what I have come to know and believe: although it is very difficult to hear and receive for some, every single event and experience and person that you have encountered was divinely orchestrated, and you are exactly where you need to be *right now*.

It is my desire throughout this book to express my understanding of who you are, why you are here, and what you are capable of. You will understand the content of this book if it is the right time for you to read it. If you do not resonate with the words of this book, gently place it on the shelf or in your library and return to it when you are ready. You will know.

I have always desired to live my life purpose. I don't do anything that I don't have a reason or process for doing. I am very talented at taking a routine job and making it easier, faster, and more fun. If I cannot do that, I stop doing that activity. Pretty simple.

CHAPTER 2

WHO ARE YOU? UNDERSTANDING WHO AND WHAT YOU ARE

You are a vibrational being. Everything that you can see, taste, touch, hear, smell, and feel is vibrating energy. This has been proven by modern science and agreed upon throughout the academic community worldwide. Everything—people, animals, cars, oceans, clouds, apples, you name it—is vibrating energy. We are beginning to understand more about our environment than we ever have before. The components and structures of all matter and material objects are based on the various speed of vibrating objects. Living objects, such as animals and human beings, have an awareness at a level that varies by the species.

For example, snails have an awareness level that provides locomotion, direction, and the ability to sustain life; however, if I *tell* one to get out of my way, it does not respond in a way that appears to be life-preserving. For this reason, I say that a snail has an awareness of doing or existing, but it does not have an awareness of or ability to communicate with me. My dog, on the other hand, understands me when I say the word *treat.* That's the only thing I have to say to cause her to immediately perk up, start wagging her tail, and jump up and down until she gets the treat. This level of awareness leads me to believe that my dog is more "aware" than a snail, but she is not aware in the same way that I am aware, or she would bypass me and get her own treats at her convenience. Some may call this intelligence, and that would be accurate, but for this book I am referring to understanding and processing experiences as awareness.

Throughout this book I will refer to awareness as unconscious or conscious. Conscious awareness is self-directed, and unconscious awareness is life-preserving awareness. Most if not all creatures will defend themselves to prevent harm and death. Most if not all have defense mechanisms and self-preserving strategies that are passed down from generation to generation. Skunks spray a foul-smelling liquid when confronted with a fearful experience. Human beings respond to disrespectful coworkers or a burglar in a way that prompts self-survival. Some will walk away, some will verbally or physically fight back, and some will complain to God or self about the undesired event. People respond to each experience in a programmed manner. We call it the fight-or-flight response, a subconscious defense mechanism that the individual was taught, imitates, or acquires once introduced to the earth environment.

I have read studies suggesting that many responses and defense mechanisms are passed along genetically and are present even if not necessarily experienced during this lifetime.

So we know that there are multiple levels of awareness, understanding, and intelligence, especially within the human species. We are living during exciting times, where science and technology are revealing capabilities that previously were unimaginable and thought impossible. In addition to the various levels of awareness, human beings have multiple emotions expressed at each level of awareness. A sad ten-year-old may retreat to solitude or laugh in discomfort when confronted with a difficult emotion, whereas a twenty-year-old may lash out, physically act out, or cry over the same emotion. People express emotion in various ways, and humanity has developed a relatively agreed-upon set of unacceptable emotional behaviors that are punishable or require medical intervention when present and acted upon. Current understanding of human behavior is expanding, and human behavior has been studied for thousands of years in many disciplines. Self-development gurus have added immensely to my understanding of human behavior when medical understanding was limited.

Many years ago, I became aware that I did not have a lot of respect for people I knew. I did not understand why, but I knew that I did not respect the advice, instruction, or criticism of many people unless they were living the life that I believed represented success. I started looking for female role models and found only certain qualities I could admire. I had a difficult time finding any one individual I could regard as "successful" and wanted to be like.

During this time, the internet was becoming readily available worldwide, and information was free and equally available. I started searching for people who modeled a successful life—people who were high achievers, kind, happy, wealthy, independent, intelligent, and living a life of freedom. I came across self-development and inspirational books and information, and my life was never the same. Once I found this genre, I was hooked.

I never had a lot of relationships with people other than my immediate family. During this time of my life, I was a new mother and college student so I didn't have time for anyone or anything other than me and my family. When I started studying successful people whom I respected based on their achievements, I saw a pattern emerge. It appeared that character traits and behaviors were extremely important and consistent within this group of studied people. I remember standing in the shower listening to Jim Rohn on YouTube and hearing him say, "It's not about what you get; it's about who you become in the process." This resonated with me, and I realized at that moment that if I wanted to have all the success of the people I was studying, I would need to develop the character traits and habits that they demonstrated.

The reason I bring up character traits and behaviors and habits is because I am going to show you that they are all related to vibrational energy at various levels of awareness. Throughout this book I will refer to successful people and contributions they have made in an attempt to help my readers understand and process the content. I do this because that is how I started connecting the dots to understanding human behavior and patterns that guided me to what I believe *is* the purpose of this life—alignment.

Human emotion and behavior have been studied throughout the world throughout time, and all the great philosophers have contributed to the whole with their consistent, dedicated attention to understanding the details and patterns of life in an effort to understand human existence. I have studied people. I have studied masters. I have studied self-development gurus, and I have studied most, if not all, the great philosophers. I have studied religion and spirituality, yoga and meditation. I have experienced adulthood, motherhood, various relationships, various careers and patterns. In modern-day terms, I have identified algorithms within my mind that gave me the most absolute best highs of my life. They are currently considered as aha moments. My addiction to learning led me to the understanding of why it became an addiction. The aha moments provided little shots of chemicals inside my brain and body known as endorphins, which are essentially my own pharmaceutical agents of happiness. In the same way that extreme sport athletes take their abilities and achievements to the next level, chemicals produced in the brain of a knowledge-seeking junkie produce abilities and achievements otherwise known as genius-level. The word *genius* has been represented by thought leaders for centuries and remains quite a fantastic accomplishment. People have long argued the origin of a genius's ability. I am here to offer the relationship of an individual's life purpose, mastery level abilities, successful lifestyles, various addictions, and undeniable miraculous abilities. Alignment. It's all about alignment. Unconscious alignment. Conscious alignment. Spiritual alignment. Vibrational alignment. Chakra alignment. Success alignment. Alignment. It's *all* about awareness, consciousness seeking alignment or itself. Energy seeking energy through energy. Alignment seeking alignment through alignment. God seeking god through god. Source seeking source through source.

While this may be very confusing to some, I know there will be readers who just "get it." I will do my best to explain and provide various methods of understanding, but keep reading even if you do not fully understand or grasp the concepts that I provide. I am aware that my thinking, processing and understanding are from my perspective, and I am the only one with my exact childhood, programming, experiences, events, traumas, achievements, education, and collected ability to process all the components in the manner that I have processed them. However, I feel that it is a good representation of the collective components that have led me to the understanding that alignment is who we are and why we are here. A more understandable concept may be God (consciousness) or source is who we essentially are in human form (matter), and alignment (connection) is why we are here.

Let that sink in. Process it as long as you need to. Then continue reading to find out how I came to that conclusion and the process to get there. If you do not fully understand, agree, or need a map guiding you from where you are to the place where preparation meets opportunity, then this book is meant for you.

CHAPTER 3

HOW YOUR MIND AND BODY WORK

The human body has been studied for centuries and is yet to be completely understood, but what we do know is that the brain is a complex computer that also functions as a receiver. Just like a radio tower, our brain receives information and translates it into thought. Thoughts evoke emotion, and emotion dictates our decisions and habits. What's interesting is the concept that our vibration directly impacts the information that we receive into our thinking mind, and thus the thoughts received are directly proportional to the vibration being given off. This is known as the law of attraction. Essentially, we receive, vibrationally, what we give off in the form of thoughts and ideas.

When you were born, you were vibrating at a high level. As you started growing up, you were bombarded with opinions, beliefs, and rules from your parents, extended family, friends, peers, and those in authority. The majority of this information was downloaded into your mind/computer prior to the age of seven. Unfortunately, most do not understand that they are running programs in their minds that are essentially directing their behavior. They think they have free will and are making all their own decisions. This is difficult to see for the first time. However, it is true.

We have both a conscious and a subconscious mind. The subconscious mind runs automatically with the programs that it has been provided, just outside the obvious conscious control. This happens a lot when we are driving our car to the store. We get there and can't remember going through the town or passing certain areas. The subconscious mind took over while the thinking mind was busy. This is a very valuable tool most of the time. It is not valuable when the subconscious plays a program that we do not wish to continue. For example, if we dislike certain family members because they are obnoxious and rude yet we continue to go eat lunch with them every Sunday, we are allowing the subconscious programming to play the record of going places we do not want to go because that is what we have always done. So clearly, there are times when we emotionally feel a tug or a feeling that we do not like, but what is the body actually telling us?

The human body has a vast set of emotional set points, which range from joy, knowledge, empowerment, and freedom to guilt, unworthiness, jealousy, anger, blame, and disappointment, to name a few. We have all felt these emotions, but did you realize that your thoughts created them? When our body produces an emotion, that is our guide to pay attention. It could be that you are doing a routine, undesired activity out of habit or from fear of hurting someone's feelings, or you may not be doing a desired action that your inner being knows you need to do to move on to the next stage of life for you. Regardless, for this chapter, it is only important that you realize that your body has an internal GPS system that is constantly an indicator of being on or off your path. Our emotions vary day to day and situation to situation; however, we are in control and are responsible for maintaining our own emotional set point. Our set point, also known as point of attraction, is whatever we put focus on. It could be a good thought or a happy idea. It could also be a painful thought or bad situation that we just cannot get over. Whatever it is that we are thinking about also produces an equal emotion about that thought. It is very important to guard your thoughts every day because what you think, you become.

When I was a little girl, I pretty much mastered the art of self-soothing. I playfully twisted my hair between my thumb and fingers, I held my thumb closed up inside my fist, and occasionally I rocked back and forth or crossed my legs and moved my upper leg to an invisible ballad. This behavior continues still today on occasion. In addition, I learned how to use the temperature of water in a bathtub to regulate and soothe sickness and bad vibes. I have used a bathtub my whole life to regulate myself without an understanding of the vibrational origin and why this appeared to always "fix" me. If you were to close your eyes right now, sit very still and focus your attention to your shoulders, and then move your attention down the length of your arms to your palms and then into your fingertips, you would be able to feel a pulsation or tingle. This energy is as real as the nose on your face, and it can be channeled in many ways to create new and improved thoughts and ideas. We will get into that deeper very soon, but for now, it is important that you understand the concept that you are a vibrational being and you are in control of the reality that you create in the future.

In addition to the vibrational mass of energy known as your physical body, you also have a computerlike brain, which uses your senses to translate the environment into understandable content and meaning. Your brain is a programmable computer system that far exceeds that of any known technology of our time. It has the ability to assess, diagnose, plan, implement, and evaluate the environment and signals being transmitted in and around its receiver. The level of reception depends on the broadcasting frequency, just like a radio tower. Abraham Hicks suggests this is similar to a radio station broadcasting on 99.5 FM. Unless your receiver is tuned in to the same exact channel, you will not receive the broadcast at all or not in an understandable manner. However, there are various frequencies always being broadcasted to our receiver, and the transmitter is always active. This phenomenon is very difficult to scientifically study; however, studies are underway and attempting to describe the physical alterations and manifestations from focused thought and intention. More on this to come.

The human body is a phenomenal system with capabilities beyond our current understanding. Some of you are like me and have always known this at some level. Depending on my mood and environment, I always felt as if I was superhuman but could not nor did I have the ability to relay this thought or understanding to myself, much less to anyone else. In the same thought, I also felt as if I was invisible to the world and of no significant importance when I contemplated the vastness and complexity of this human realm and world. Something deep within us knows there is more to the human experience than what we have experienced. That we are powerful beyond our own understanding. That we are more than the physical representations with limits that we interact with every day. The desire for clarity in our own personal lives, as well as the human species, gives rise to a longing for more answers and more revelations. Understanding human potential and capabilities within ourselves is the next step in human evolution. This expansion is a result of the dreamer's and idealist's desire to escape the mundane.

CHAPTER 4

WHAT YOU ARE SEEKING
IS A FEELING

Ultimately, I think we would all agree that we are all seekers. Seeking something better—whether it be success or happiness, purpose or meaning. We are attempting to understand why we are here and what we are here to do. I figured out a long time ago that I wanted to know why things were the way they were. How things operated and what factors were concrete and what was manipulatable. Like I said earlier, I figured out early in life that I could use warm bathwater to feel better. It took a long time for me to understand the premise behind this and how it actually made a difference in my physical body, but I have a good understanding now. It's interesting that even as a little girl, I understood there were factors that I had control over to make myself feel better. I now realize that as a vibrational being coming into contact with hot and cold, light and dark, wet and dry, demonstrates a change or difference in my physical state of being for the worse or for the better. When I use the words *worse* or *better*, I am generalizing positive and negative feelings and responses. A positive response would be considered a good response, and a negative or worse feeling would be considered bad. A warm bath felt good to me, while a cold-water bath made me internally shake and feel discomfort. I remember this quite vividly because I sat in a bath of cool water many times during my childhood. My body was very sensitive to the environment, and I often demonstrated illness, causing a fever. At that time, a doctor recommended to my parents to have me sit in a tub of lukewarm to cool bathwater to help my body bring my fever back to the desired temperature. I suppose this worked because I am still here, but the memories are pretty vivid when I recall these events. I did not like the way I felt sitting in the cool bathwater. I do not have any remembrance of not feeling well or how I felt before and after; all I remember is the experience of sitting in the tub of cold water and not wanting to be there.

My experience of physical sensations is unique to me as I am the only one capable of fully experiencing my own network of nerve endings throughout my sensory organs; however, I know my experience of certain sights, sounds, and feelings seems very intense to me. I almost feel like I am in overload frequently. For this reason I retreat from any experience or person that doesn't feel good to me. I never knew that I was experiencing vibrations that did not resonate with me, but now I do. I was always a pretty happy girl. Even as I grew into a woman, I remained happy and focused on my inner desires to serve and love. I enjoyed meeting new people and identifying challenges to conquer. I spent very little time maintaining relationships that did not feed me or nourish my soul. It seemed that I tolerated certain people only if they brought something positive to my or my children's lives. Otherwise, I dismissed that situation or person as if I never knew them. I had no desire to talk about them over and over or to get people to join with my opinion. Sure, there were a few who *really* got under my skin. I mean, they simply were rude and wrong in my opinion. I despised their behavior, and I had big issues with their inconsistency. One comes to mind as I write this, and let me tell you, he was a doozy. From a child I always had a conflict with people bossing me around. I understood parental influence and love regardless of how inconsistent and irrational I thought they were. You see, I had this gift, and it was probably my greatest asset … I was very observant. I had a way of observing people and their behavior over a long span of time and then dissecting the patterns or inconsistencies. Anytime someone spoke, taught, preached, or praised a behavior, I listened. I also watched people closely, and over time I started seeing inconsistencies that I did not understand. Some taught love but would not show love to certain people. Some taught certain behaviors were sin, while going home and doing very similar unhealthy practices. It didn't take long for me to start rebelling against these people. Then it escalated to almost all authority figures. I didn't understand my behavior, but nonetheless it was present, and I had very little control over it no matter what I tried. For a long time I just stayed away from people who made me feel this weird feeling inside when I was around them. I would try to like them, but every time I got around them, my body physically rejected them by getting very excited, anxious, and shaky. As I became an adult, I thought this feeling was intimidating, and I greatly disliked being around people who intimidated me. I have come to realize this feeling now is better known as a vibrational wave pattern of judgment. Judgment? Couldn't be. Yes, I had come to finally realize many years later that the intimidating behavior I had grown so aggravated with, I had developed. I could not stand people who were racist or prejudiced. I disliked animal abusers as much or more than people abusers. I developed a strong dislike for anyone who showed favoritism or preached their way was the right way. The next twenty years of my adult life were focused directly on learning how to dismantle and "fix" all the negative, racist, ignorant people on this planet. Little did I know that I was becoming the most intimidating of all. I was trying to force people to see their ignorance by showing them I knew the way.

I can't quite laugh at this yet, but I'm hopeful it's coming. Acceptance was necessary. Accepting that the very things we stand against, we bring energy and attention to. You see, the universe is set up with certain laws. Meaning what you love and desire, you draw to yourself. What you dislike and focus on eliminating, you draw in to your own experience. The very power used to keep it within my awareness was the power that caused it to come into my life. By the time I was thirty-five years old, I had emotionally withdrawn from nearly every part of society. I believed I was more intelligent than most and recognized that getting away from anyone and anything that made me feel negative or intimidated actually worked. I also made it a lifelong cause to call out every single belief or behavior that I felt was cruel, judgmental, disconnecting, or separating. All I was doing was calling bigger and "badder" behaviors into my life to judge. This repetitious cycle continued until I legitimately did not want to be around anyone or anything that I found fault with.

I just couldn't get far enough away from all the junk in the world that annoyed me. In fact, I found it everywhere I looked. I began to believe that I was the *only* person around who actually understood life. This left me empty and consumed for an answer. As you can see from the introduction in this book, I read and studied every book and potential way to find happiness and set the world straight. I had eliminated all real human contact in search of perfection and answers, which only created more avenues of knowledge and more concepts to understand.

We live in an expanding universe. This is possible through desire and contrast. We cannot know love without experiencing heartbreak. We cannot fully experience life without experiencing death and separation from our loved ones. I learned this nugget of wisdom in the most exquisitely painful way. Life has a way of giving us the desires of our heart. You see, when I was twenty years old, I got on my knees in prayer, and I called out to my God with the purest of intentions and the most unbelievable strength of the emotion of love. I asked for wisdom. The wisdom of Solomon. In fact, I asked for more wisdom than Solomon was given, and the Bible stated that he had more wisdom than any other man. I now understand that the only way to acquire wisdom on any given matter is to fully experience it. Wisdom is the end result of a painful experience once the sting of pain has subsided. *Wow.* Who knew? Clearly, I have received exactly what I asked for, and it has come at a cost that almost consumed me out of this world. It was never another human being who was my enemy. It was never intimidating bullies whom I struggled to get away from. It was human consciousness experiencing growth. It was my expanding desires, my consciousness, intersecting with my contrast, resulting in expansion. For all the quantum physicists and scientific geniuses, this was the physical experience of energy in action ($E = MC^2$), from conceptual thought into manifestation in physical form and now into the written word. It was *me* experiencing *me* and reflecting off every person and experience to cause *me* to expand. When any one of us grows and expands our conscious awareness, the entire human species expands as well.

Okay, I am aware that my understanding and explanation sound a bit bizarre. Nonetheless, it is my best effort of explaining my truth. Overall, it has become more clear that we are all here for a purpose. The purpose that I conclude is a bit funner, less stressful, and more like an unfolding than an accumulation of any descriptions that I have studied. We are all vibrational beings experiencing life through our physical senses. Our senses allow us to navigate, experience, and enjoy the physical aspects of life. Our internal GPS system or thoughts, emotions, and feelings are our guide to create more of what we want and identify what we don't. The negative feelings and aspects of life that we want to turn our heads to are better known to me now as contrast. Once I learned this tidbit, everything changed for me. Our bodies' ability to identify what we want and what we don't want to experience is exactly why we are here in this dimension, scouring around this big rock flying through space, searching for meaning. This is expansion. This is growth. This is evolution. Understanding the vibrational aspect of who we are, coupled with the inner ability of our body system, gives us just a taste of what is possible. Once you fully understand the processes by which our human existence functions at the foundational level, buckle up … ordinary life is over.

CHAPTER 5

WHY YOU DO WHAT YOU DO

Let's look at human behavior from a different perspective. Imagine yourself as a circle of light. Now imagine the yin and yang symbol in two-tone color within your circle of light. The darker areas are part of the whole as well as the lighter areas. The complete picture would be considered a whole picture. The same is demonstrated in human behavior. We label our behavior as good or bad. Right and wrong. When in reality, it is all behavior from various perspectives. There is a human agreement that murder is not a good behavior; however, murder has been a sacrificial act in some religions of various cultures and praised. With this thought in mind, it is possible to understand the many aspects and thoughts fueling human behavior and experiences. They are almost understandable even if we disagree. How can this be?

When we assess human behavior from our own personal perception, it is difficult to understand others' behavior, yet when we start observing from a broader perspective why people do what they do, it becomes much more clear and understandable. In understanding, we can form a basis as to how to rectify and direct desired human behavior. With this in mind, let's look at human behavior from a vibrational standpoint. If we are vibrational beings, meaning, energy vibrating at various speeds, then it's possible that the speed of vibration is directly related to the thoughts and behaviors of the individual being. As we discussed before, our vibration sends out a signal to the universe, and our receiving tower, our brain, receives a responding, similar signal or thought. This thought produces equivalent emotions within our physical body. This law of attraction event is as consistent as gravity.

Scale of Emotions
1. Joy/Knowledge/Empowerment/Freedom/Love/ Appreciation
2. Passion
3. Enthusiasm
4. Positive Expectation/Belief
5. Optimism
6. Hopefulness
7. Contentment
8. Boredom
9. Pessimism
10. Frustration/Irritation/Impatience

11. "Overwhelment"
12. Disappointment
13. Doubt
14. Worry
15. Blame
16. Discouragement
17. Anger
18. Revenge
19. Hatred/Rage
20. Jealousy
21. Insecurity/Guilt/Unworthiness
22. Fear/Grief/Depression/Despair/Powerlessness

After looking at the scale of emotions provided, it makes sense that the higher the vibration, the higher the emotion, and the lower the vibration, the lower the emotion. So it is safe to say that if I am a vibrational being experiencing life in a physical body, then the level of vibration within my body is responsible for the receiving vibration, which is translated into thoughts and emotions, thus directing my thinking and decision-making. In essence, my decisions are directly related to the emotions and feelings that I am feeling when I make those decisions. If I am vibrating at the level of jealousy or hatred, then my decisions and resulting actions will be equivalent to that. This explains the concept of an "eye for an eye" (Matthew 5:36 NIV) or "Do unto them as you would have them do unto you" (Luke 6:31 NIV). Another term I like to use is karma. What I get is what I deserve. This is very difficult for a lot of people to digest. How can I be receiving all this drama and bad luck if I didn't do anything to deserve it?

I have a good friend. He means the world to me. When I met him, I thought he was the most perfect man and father that I had ever met. As time progressed, I started seeing him battle situations that seemed very unfair. He did not have a reckless bone in his body. In fact, he was one of the most up-front, genuine, kindhearted givers I had ever met. Yet I watched him get hit every month with a different set of unlucky circumstances. He would laugh and say, "Nothing surprises me." He did not get mad or criticize the situation; he just dealt with it. I am a connector. I like puzzles, and I love experiencing aha moments when a neural connection is newly formed with new information. So over time I observed his lifestyle, behavior, and experiences, and I saw interesting patterns emerge. Although he did not have any negative intentions, he received undesired experiences in two critical areas. He could not understand the stroke of bad luck or why people were acting like they were. However, I could see quite clearly. No, it had nothing to do with his bad or intentional actions to these people. It was quite the opposite. He had withdrawn certain behavior, and they were upset with him that he was no longer making their world more comfortable. This greatly interested me. So not only do we reap what we sow; we also reap the leftover momentum from people in our lives who take more than they give. When we allow unwanted behaviors from others or we overlook unpleasant behavior within ourselves or within others, we are not helping anyone. We are actually causing harm to both parties in the long run. If something doesn't feel right about a situation, it's not. Learning how to feel our way through each situation using our internal GPS system will produce much more desired outcomes.

This expanded my awareness and gave me a better, fuller perspective to evaluate and assess multiple areas. A good example is in learning the English language. Early in the developmental process, a child learns one-syllable words and is then able to communicate with others who understand what they are expressing. The guesswork disappears, and the ability to speak the exact desire in words greatly speeds up the getting. However, over time, the child has learned the language but finds that when desires arise and the child expresses the desire to the parent, they are told "no" or "not now." This confuses the child until the child is able to fully explain why he or she desires the item or the parent is able to explain why they think the desire is not available or in the child's best interest. Good communication with appropriate language is essential for all parties to feel expressed and understood.

When more of the population begin to hear and process the concept of humans as vibrational beings over static material beings, a new way of understanding will emerge. With this concept in mind, let's further this by suggesting that there is a shift taking place as I write this and as you read this very book. A shift in consciousness across the globe. We are beginning to see a transition from doing to a state of being. It's no secret that the traditional nine-to-five, Monday-through-Friday workweek is just not meeting people's standards anymore. People are wanting more freedom from time-consuming jobs to spend more time with people they enjoy doing what they love. In the past this was considered leisure time and, to some workaholics, lazy behavior. The mind-set that one must work hard to achieve success is outdated and inconsistent with the trends of online ecommerce and work-from-anywhere modalities. Advertisements are promoting less physical work and more intelligent use of modern technology. In addition to the reluctance of the currently hardworking, traditional population to accept the new breed referred to as millennials, we are also experiencing a shift in modern health care from synthetic chemicals and surgical intervention to placebo-effect medication and distance energy healing. Not only has yoga become popular in the West for various reasons, but it has its grasps in our university and younger populations.

So what is going on? What is this shift we are experiencing within our minds and visibly within our physical reality? Its alignment. Vibrational alignment. It's what it's all about. It's what the entire earth and creation is moaning for. It is a shift. More like a birth into a new earth and a new heaven experience. There was a consciousness, the feminine quality of being, that expanded with the masculine quality of doing, and the material world that we experience with our physical senses and process with our minds was made manifest. Out of this expansion, we received animal and plant life, as well as human life, all residing on and in Mother Earth. The masculine quality of logic and reasoning produced amazing technologies, and the feminine quality of intuition, nurturing, and creativity brought the emotion and pleasure of art and its mastery. It is almost overwhelming to fully evaluate and process the natural beauty of our planet, as well as the amazing physical and academic achievements of our species. The artists, the musicians, the athletic performers, the extreme sport extremists, the self-development gurus, and the exquisite beauty and brains residing in LA, New York, and Nashville are all manifestations from the nonphysical. The alignment of the inner components is being expressed throughout the outer components. The kingdom of heaven is within.

CHAPTER 6

MASCULINE AND FEMININE ENERGY

Human existence has evolved from very primitive states to quite complex beings over the past thousands of years. The individual experience is becoming ever visible and profound while remaining quite primitive in some aspects. The earth and creation are altogether a mixture of feminine and masculine properties manifesting into what we know as the human *being* and human existence. The feminine qualities found within the earth, as well as the human being, include intuition, creativity, and nurturing, while the masculine properties are logic, reasoning, and action. Each individual has both feminine and masculine counterparts. These characteristics are fundamental and apparent as survival instincts of prehistoric relationships; however, there has been a plethora of variations, percentages, and challenges consistently evolving in both male and female individuals. Modern-day relationships are taking on new traditions, and old traditions are falling away. Clearly this is not welcome in a large majority of the population; however, the fact remains that the momentum of change is happening whether the majority agree or not.

For the sake of expansion, I will let the naysayers and the closet sinners do all the judging and rationalizing on male/female relationships and what is acceptable and what is forbidden; but for this book, I will clarify my understanding of how the feminine and masculine qualities have been showing up within individuals—as well as in my life—for centuries. Make note that there is a very real expansion and growth within this realm and has been for some time now. The masculine qualities of logic and reasoning are definitely beneficial and have been evolving society throughout time. The physical characteristics of men are well-known, including strength and functionality in comparison to the smaller female physical structure. This has served its purpose as the earth and all species evolved into current-day reality. As a female and from my life experience, I am a very emotion-focused, feeling individual. I base most of my decisions on feelings, and a lot of times, I am confronted with conflict for taking an emotional, personal stance different from that of the general population. It was not until I started studying human behavior and character that I identified that my belief system and inner feelings did not line up. Often, I behaved a certain way, and other people did not agree with my behavior as appropriate. For example, I love being a woman. Sure, it's crossed my mind a time or two how it would feel to be in a man's body and experience life from that perspective, but essentially I find contentment and appreciation that I am the receiver and weaker physical being in my intimate relationship. Now, with that in mind, power is a feeling that I enjoy a significant amount of time. Powerlessness is not only unpleasant but unwanted. Because the feminine characteristics encompass intuition, compassion, and nurturing, it has been thought and passed on from generation to generation that the feminine is the weaker gender. I am finding that the belief pattern of feminine as weak is a false premise and occasionally used to curtail feminine power. The feminist movement is a direct demonstration of contrast expressed as repressed feminine power, and when seen through the lens of logic and reasoning (masculine characteristics), it appears to be rebellious and masculine. In reality you could say it is; however, feminine power can be reclaimed with and without picketing and signs and marches. Unfortunately, due to the worldwide belief pattern and vibration, these avenues have been the path of least resistance. The masculine energy continues to purposely resist the feminine rise of power; however, the fact remains that the momentum has been underway for a century and is being exhibited in leadership positions, such as social media executives, various powerful CEO positions, and the overall global vibration. This is interesting to me, and I have spent significant energy, internally, contemplating the amplitude and potential changes moving forward. My depth of understanding takes me back to consciousness before materialization into form. The feminine and masculine energy has always been, and it is the original combined energy of consciousness. Now, I propose some interesting thoughts and direction from my perspective on the person as a whole, containing both feminine and masculine properties. Every individual you meet, including yourself, has masculine and feminine energy. Like a magnet, we attract and repel energy. I consider myself very feminine; however, I am more feminine around certain people. This was confusing to me till I understood the vibrational offering that I was sending out. I consider myself to be 80/20 or 70/30, with feminine qualities dominating most of the time. When my intimate partner is present, I am clearly 80/20. He is extremely logical and masculine, which seems to put my energy in a high percentage of creativity and compassion for life. Almost kidlike. My decision-making capacity of logic and reasoning dissipates, and I fully rely on him as the logic and reasoning presence when we are together. I sing and dance and melt onto his lap for hours at a time. There are days when we do absolutely nothing but sit together or fish or talk deeply for hours upon hours. It is quite breathtaking when I contemplate the complete contentment I feel internally when he is around. Almost like a feel-good drug addiction. However, when he is not present, my sense of security and safety heightens, and my child-like presence diminishes. Some might conclude this is characteristic of a split personality feature or two different women. However, it is merely the magnetic pull that we have on each other when we are in physical close proximity. When he is not in the same location or town that I am in, I can still feel him, and when I focus directly on him, I can feel the strength of our attraction wax and wane. It's quite magical. But there is no denying that the personality that is present when he is within close range is altered from the adult female version that I have lived and demonstrated my whole adult life. Once I recognized this difference, I started focusing my thoughts toward him throughout the day when I completed my day's tasks, and it seemed that he received this attention and returned the attention until we were back together for the day.

The large majority of my life has been spent observing and assessing the environment while making decisions focused on my desired end result. I spent most of my childhood playing alone at my parents' home and surrounding areas. This created a great amount of focus and reasoning. My strong feminine energy allowed my logic and reasoning characteristics to surface equally. This allowed me to make decisions about my future as well as the future of my children as a provider and protector, while maintaining the compassionate, creative, and nurturing mothering character. I can see this throughout my entire teenage years and adulthood. Until *him*. In chapter 9 on cooperative components, the reader will get to dive into some very personal life events and experiences that altered my perception and focused attention, completely changing the target course of my life. However, in respect to defining and understanding the feminine and masculine energies as a whole, I just want to demonstrate what each energy looks and feels like and its characteristics that can be altered, subject to environmental factors.

People act differently around certain people. This behavior confused me, and I judged people for a long time based on the personality changes that I witnessed in various environments. I thought people were fake until I witnessed and experienced the very evident changes within myself around certain people and certain environments. Once I understood the experiences and the energy exchanges that were taking place, I understood the feelings that resulted when I was around certain people and places. Now that you have a little insight to what is actually going on within you as your environment and energy change, you will be able to read the emotions and vibes that you are experiencing and why they are absent or present.

I am a thinker. I spend a significant amount of time observing and reading the environment. I no longer make decisions based on rationalization or logic. I listen to my internal emotions and interpret the vibrations that I receive based on how I feel about each person, each thought, and each environment before I commit to just about anything. Once in a while, I make a decision to go somewhere or not go somewhere without checking in with my GPS indicator, but I can assure you that it does not take long for me to identify that something is off if I made a decision that contradicts my acceptable vibration change. I am not willing to consciously put myself in an environment that makes me feel bad or weird or unwanted. There are a million reasons why we pick up on vibrations that feel off to us, but does it really matter? Any vibration that leads my inner GPS system to indicate the presence of a lower vibration, such as anger, jealousy, lack of safety, or distrust, is automatically a red flag, and I pay attention.

With that in mind, I must say that there are times that I misread people and the environment. I am still learning to validate, understand, and interpret each situation, but I know the people and environments that resonate with me, and I will spend the rest of my life attempting to align with that very feeling and the people and places that match my high vibration. The hardest part of the energy exchange that I have experienced is when I am in an environment that requires my full attention, logic, and reasoning skills, but I'm with my masculine counterpart, which usually encompasses my full attention and provides the reasoning and logic.

This challenge was initially hard for me to understand and caused me to seclude myself from the rest of the world because I did not understand how to manage my vibration at a consistent level.

For example, my partner and I made a trip early in our relationship to Arizona for a business retreat for my health-care company. We arrived at the airport and made our way through security and to our terminal with absolutely no stress or inconvenience. Once we arrived at the terminal, we both decided that we needed one last bathroom break before boarding the plane. As soon as we returned to the terminal, the boarding entrance was closed, and the flight staff refused to let us board the plane. We had prepurchased tickets for the flight, and the boarding cutoff was still minutes away, yet the flight crew reported that all seats were taken and that we were replaced when we did not board during the allotted time frame. This was definitely not a pleasant experience; at that moment, however, I clearly remember laughing about it like elementary-age children and walking away to find another flight to Arizona. We made our way to the servicing airline customer service counter and reported the mix-up. We requested a same-day flight to my company retreat if possible and were willing to wait at the airport till seats were available. So, like a game of musical chairs, we sat at each terminal flight to Arizona to see if we would be welcomed onto that hour's flight. At the end of each flight's boarding call, we gleamed like kids, while absorbing all the fun, positive energy available anticipating a seat. Hour after hour we sat patiently at each flight terminal until the final flight of the day was boarding around 9:00 p.m. The entire day had been spent in the most wonderful, dreamlike state of fun and exciting anticipation. As the flight attendant finalized the seat availability for this last flight, we noticed there were eight additional people waiting for a seat. Six people were not going to get on this last flight, and we had zero reservation that we would be included in that six. And then, as we had anticipated, they called both our names over the intercom to quickly claim the last two seats of the flight. I giggled with delight, and he winked at me as he grabbed our luggage and I partially danced all the way to our seats.

We arrived late in Arizona and had to get a ride to the retreat center an hour away. The transportation provision was not active again till the following morning, and I had missed the keynote speaker, B. J. Miller, MD, whom I had desired to meet and connect with after hearing his TED talk and personal life and career history. Nonetheless, I was not a bit frustrated with myself or the airline. We had arrived, and the magic remained throughout the remainder of the trip, till we returned home.

I do not remember that much about the event or the guest speakers. I learned very little if any new material, and my career did not benefit one penny's worth. But let me tell you, the memories from that trip are etched deeply in my mind as one of the most amazing feelings that I can tap into at any time. The energy of the experience left me with a point of energy that I can return to anytime I desire and take away the best, smile-producing thought imaginable. I was unable to argue or complain during that whole trip. It was insanity inside my head as I attempted to attend conference classes and pay attention to the information being presented. I could not do it. I could not separate my playful, whimsical personality from the mature, professional colleague that I was one week prior. I believe I would have made the initial flight, arrived on time, and attended all the events and had a beneficial time had I gone alone. Probably what the company intended. However, the masculine and feminine energy that produces logical, rational, adult decision-making was not only absent from my grasp; it was unnecessary. But then I guess that depends on whom you ask.

This is merely one personal example of my understanding and experience of the feminine and masculine energy exchange demonstrated within myself and how they vary based on the environment. Whom I surround myself with greatly affects my energy, including the degree of masculine and feminine energy necessary for that relationship. There are times when it is very difficult for me to reason and think logically and then document it effectively. If the environment is too loud or there are too many people present, I have a difficult time staying focused and attentive to the task at hand. As a nurse practitioner, I do a significant amount of dictation after I see a patient. Typically I take notes throughout the patient encounter, and once I am secluded in a quiet environment, I am able to recount my assessment diagnosis and plan and any interventions, prescriptions, or instructions necessary and document accordingly.

With nearly 7 billion human beings alive on this planet, give or take, it goes to reason that there is quite a mixture of beings with various percentages of the feminine and masculine energies present. For example, the alpha male is a good example of strong masculine energy. The alpha male will demonstrate a variety of characteristics and personality traits; however, the logic, reasoning, and action-oriented behavior is quite strong and dominant. I would rate a typical alpha male as 80 to 90 percent masculine energy and 10 to 20 percent feminine energy. Of course this will vary, but for the sake of understanding the energy mix, I will use 80/20. This mix makes a lot of sense why alpha males tended to lean toward similar types of female partners in the past, but changes are underway as the population moves more toward individual wholeness, and I like to call it the mirror effect. People enjoy the company of other people who have similarities that they themselves have. Gym rats like gym rats. Hikers like hikers. Gamers like gamers. Football fans like other football fans (typically of the same team). So it makes a lot of sense that like attracts like.

The mirror effect is something a little different, though. Over the years I have noticed changes in whom I surround myself with. In fact, I don't spend much time with anyone other than myself and a few select people whom I resonate with. By resonate, I mean, have similar likes, experiences, and beliefs. Because of the many transformations I have undergone during my lifetime, I have found it difficult to make and maintain friendships. Not because I am antisocial but because I have a hard time maintaining conversations that do not interest me. I guess through high school I managed to get by, but since I became an adult, I have only been interested in studying philosophy and learning how to overcome the human condition. It seems that there is a small percentage of truly successful people on the planet, and the remaining population struggle on a daily basis to meet their own needs as well as their families' needs. Advances in technology have made communication and knowledge readily available, yet people seem so overwhelmed with knowledge and options that they can't make decisions or stay focused on important topics and tasks. Distraction has become the norm, but so have shorter workweeks and more independence in the workplace.

The relationship that people have with others, especially their intimate partners, appears to me like a mirror. We cross paths with another individual, and for that moment or month or year, we mirror our adoration for each other, but at some point we begin experiencing conflict, opposition, different habits, and various wounds that cripple the relationship and cause stress. Some overcome and pursue understanding during these situations; others continue the relationship but discontinue the past, unpleasant experiences and find new friendships or hobbies to fill their time. Some end the relationship and begin a new life, only to repeat the same patterns with the next partner. I believe this is due to the vibrational point of attraction that the individual maintains without intervention and understanding of this pattern. No change will take place, and death will be the only relief of the physical body's resistance.

If we understand the mirror effect and the vibrational point of attraction within ourselves, we can then make some conscious intentions and changes that will alter our vibration to a more desired set point. Understanding that we are vibrational beings and that we have the ability to create a different point of attraction allows us to change our reality into a more desirable outcome. It all starts with understanding who and what we are and our ability to make intentions and decisions to alter our current state, which leads to changes in our current reality. One of the best ways to understand ourselves is to look at the people that we resonate with, the people we most often interact with and spend valuable time connecting with.

Earlier in this chapter, I gave the example of my and my partner's experience at an airport, demonstrating the various feminine and masculine energy exchanges. It is not always so glittery and sweet. There are times when the energies clash so badly that one of us has to literally leave the immediate environment or fall into significant overwhelm. Almost every time this has happened, neither one of us had the ability to catch the mood in the early stages to prevent the meltdown. The benefit of these moments does not show itself for hours, or days in some cases, but every single time, it is a mirror for both of us to see with clarity.

I'm learning that our childhood upbringing, home environment, and past and current life experiences are the only vibrational obstacles during these times. But those energetic beliefs are as powerful as the overwhelming love that is present before and after those times. I attribute this understanding to light and darkness. Light is revealing and freely flowing, while darkness is merely the absence of light. Both are visible and describable with our human senses; however, one is only present when the other is blocked or absent. This is a good example of the mirror effect within the masculine and feminine energy relationships. Attraction is real. However, attraction to another human takes on so many components because of the belief patterns and life experiences of each individual being so different. The vibration of each individual, however, remains the same and only varies when it becomes blocked or compromised. The more that I contemplate this thought, the more it resonates with me.

It is a lot easier to identify blocked-off patterns and inconsistencies in others than it is within myself, but I now understand that this is a result of a previous experience and understanding within myself. Perspective makes all the difference. Alignment increases perspective. Inspired action from alignment speeds up the time involved from experience and understanding, thus providing perspective not previously available.

Words don't teach. Only experience does. But words can offer the experience a vibrational level of understanding that alters one's perspective. Our understanding of the human experience varies, and its understanding and interpretation can be directly proportional to the vibrational alignment of the receptive being interpreting the vibration as thought. The words and thoughts that we receive and speak to others as well as to ourselves are our greatest opportunity to change our vibration to a more desirable platform. Until we master the art of thought and words, no thought and no words are our second-best option, and that is what meditation attempts to achieve. Part II of this book is aimed at mastering daily alignment in an effort to bring clarity, empowerment, joy, and appreciation for this mysterious unfolding and expansion of human consciousness.

CHAPTER 7

VIBRATIONAL ALIGNMENT
SUMMARY

Part I is all about doing what feels good every day from an unconscious perspective. Once it is understood that essentially all decisions, choices, and motivation come from the unconscious, instinct-driven mind, one can then make the conscious decision to contemplate their past, identify cooperative components, and understand their choices from a path of least resistance. Some may say, "I don't do what feels good every day; I do what I have to do to get by." And that is an extremely good example of doing what feels good or expected compared to doing something that my family or peers or community would not agree with. To not do what is expected creates an internal feeling of rejection or worry, and that does not feel good. Get it? Good.

Human existence is evolving, and finding alignment with oneself is the ultimate goal, whether conscious or unconscious. Joy, freedom, appreciation, and love all come from the vibrational alignment of self with source, and people achieve this level in various ways. Passion and drive to accomplish alignment can now be demonstrated with conscious understanding and inspired action. My personal mission statement is to empower others by setting the example of conscious, daily alignment and by demonstrating the results of living in daily alignment within my personal life expression.

My backstory will provide the path to understanding alignment and the core concepts and processes identified for my daily conscious alignment. The path of least resistance helps one to understand the various choices made to obtain desires and preferences. A desire for something is really just a desire to feel good. Least resistance means that on your life path you will encounter roadblocks at the unconscious level. These roadblocks come in the form of beliefs, patterns, and habits that we all absorbed and learned from the environment and teachings in our youth. Lack of knowledge, lack of understanding, and lack of resources are all part of each individual's journey. If you are reading this book and you have gotten this far, it is likely that you have encountered these roadblocks to success and happiness and desire to identify, understand, and implement new beliefs and thoughts to clear the resistance and achieve success.

Our lives are filled with segments of various divine encounters and components. These are the cooperative components of your life. All the people, events, experiences, sensory involvement, animals, environments, toys, and resources make up our individual cooperative components. All the cooperative components that can be identified can be grouped into positive or negative experiences or memories and understood. With understanding of our individual experiences, patterns emerge, and we then have the ability for personal change.

Who are you? You are God consciousness in physical form. The human body is the navigating device within this material world that we live in. Your emotions and feelings are your internal GPS or navigating system indicators. The level of your energy vibration equals your point of attraction, also known as the universal law of attraction. Essentially we are all transmitters, receiving and sending signals or vibrations for growth and expansion in the physical plane or realm. In the spiritual realm, it is the eternal now. In the physical realm, the space and time continuum give rise to the construct of past, present, and future. From birth into the physical realm, into a material navigating system with tools and awareness to grow and expand. All of the individual cooperative components, both positive and negative from the physical perspective, are necessary. From the spiritual perspective, all cooperative components demonstrate alignment with what is wanted or demonstrate contrast from what is not desired or wanted. Both are beneficial and bring about growth and expansion to the individual, as well as the collective human experience. Imagine a conscious awareness experiencing growth and expansion through creation of billions of individual points of attraction or perceptions.

PART II

VIBRATIONAL ALIGNMENT MASTERY

CHAPTER 8

MASTERING ALIGNMENT

Are there days when you feel like giving up? Do you feel like you are doing everything that you know to do to get where you want to go, and yet you wake up to another day exactly the same as the previous day? Consider this: "The last thing to grow on a fruit tree is the fruit."

Now that you have completed part I of this book, you should have gained an understanding of what you are, why you are here, how alignment feels within the body, and how to determine your vibrational set point by simply asking the question "How do I feel right now?" In the upcoming chapters you will be given an overview of various tools, processes, and strategies to consciously use to get into vibrational alignment. Not only is vibrational alignment the natural being's set point when flowing pure positive energy; it is also a state of bliss that can be experienced in the now. Not only are we vibrational energetic beings; we are creators. When we unblock the beliefs and patterns that cause inner resistance, we are able to flow pure positive energy, and the creation process becomes limitless. We are all essentially already using a lot of these strategies and processes in our daily lives. For the majority of the population these processes, tools, and strategies are used unconsciously. When we create unconsciously, we tend to create a reality of wanted things as well as unwanted things and scenarios within our lives. But once you understand and know this consciously, you will be able to use these tools and processes deliberately to get into daily alignment and stay there. This is where miracles happen.

For example, take Tony Robbins, the freak of nature. Whether he knows it or not (and I'm sure he does), he demonstrates alignment within his life and has developed processes to this alignment that he implements on a daily basis. His life demonstrates what some may refer to as superhuman or supernatural creative abilities. I've never met him in person, but I've watched nearly every episode and video he provided on YouTube. Clearly Tony has identified his cooperative components, and he has used them to magnify his purpose. Some of the cooperative components that I identified from his videos and audios are considered positive (mentors, right place-right time, people), and others are referred to as unpleasant events or experiences from his childhood I identify as contrast from desired situations. These undesirable and pleasant events produced memories that Tony capitalized on in a beneficial way to follow his inner guide to greatness. For those of you reading this book who are familiar with Tony Robbins, this will make sense to you. His alignment, contrast, cooperative components, and seeker mentality produced a historical, iconic figure—himself. He is the gift. Alignment is the way. He has manifested into this reality his purpose and gift to this world. A quantum leap for all humanity. That is mastery.

In mastering alignment, you will evolve. Who you are, what you create, and how it manifests into this reality will be your gift to the world. By understanding the recipe for mastery-level living, you will begin to consciously create the genuine, authentic, truest, and best version of yourself. I believe that this understanding, coupled with the experience of alignment, will bring about more mastery-level human beings just like Tony Robbins, Michael Jordan, Elon Musk, and Oprah. With the new conscious understanding and breakdown processes that follow all the attentive, mastery-level individuals will be able to master the mastery level with their own conscious, intentional application of the alignment process. Average Joes will do the impossible. Seekers will become masters. Masters will take genius to the next level. What is the next level? I do not have a word, example, or demonstrable manifestation or example at this point. However, given that thoughts produce ideas and our thoughts and ideas are manifestations from our vibrational alignment set points, I'm excited and confident that the magnitude of these potential manifestations are unlimited possibilities. A dreamlike reality. Superhuman endeavors. World peace and harmony. United borders. Love like the biblical Jesus taught and demonstrated, which made this book, my personal growth, and the expansion that is taking place as you read this very chapter.

The feelings of vibrational alignment include passion, joy, love, freedom, happiness, and empowerment at the highest level. A master at the mastery level will produce miracles by eliminating all resistance. Once we, as a species, through the collective gift of mastery-level alignment, start to experience mastery of our own personal alignment and understand its components, daily mastery will manifest across the earth like wildfire. The four-minute mile was once a dream. Impossible. But once the thought and idea downloaded from one individual's alignment, it quickly became a reality; very quickly the four-minute mile was mastered and then became a norm. So let's break down the mastery-level ability from a vibrational alignment perspective and get this information out to the world. Through the collective gift of mastery-level alignment, I offer the ideas surrounding the conscious creator and superhuman experience.

CHAPTER 9

COOPERATIVE COMPONENTS

Experiencing an understanding of the cooperative components of our personal lives will provide a key ingredient in the superhuman pie. Every life experience, our children, our parents, our siblings, our friends, every mentor, every beautiful moment, every nightmare, every bump in the road, every special pet, every home, every meeting, our school days, our college experiences, and all the good and all the bad events and experiences that you have experienced make up the cooperative components of your life.

When I say good and bad experiences, I am technically referring to the emotion that one experiences and continues to experience with the memory of that life event. You may have deep regret about a life experience decision or event. You may have unwanted emotions surrounding this event. You may not have been able to understand or explain to yourself or others how this event was beneficial. However, I am going to give you an overview of my life and some of the cooperative components that at one point I considered good and bad. In addition, I will present to you the process of understanding each of these and how I transformed each into understandable events, experiences, and memories. When everything is identified, understood, and experienced from alignment, you will unleash within yourself the most beautiful and powerful gift you can give yourself—forgiveness, the ability to essentially erase the negative emotions surrounding past events.

I experienced a magical transformation within myself as I sat in my living room contemplating one afternoon. It was a ripple effect much like the ripple formation produced in a pond after a stone is tossed into it. At the point where the stone meets the water, a transformation takes place in all possible directions as the ripple dissipates. My accumulated experiences, knowledge, and understanding have led me to a similar experience I like to call the ripple effect. The ripple effect moment activated a change within my conscious awareness in all directions of my life, including the future, past, and present. At that moment I experienced an intense overwhelming sensation that was difficult to contain within my physical body. The vibration of that ripple changed my understanding surrounding many events of my life and transformed the entire experience within me. Not only were beliefs or blockages identified; many were destroyed as pure positive energy flowed through many events, circumstances, components, and sensory perceptions across the entire life span of my past, present, and future. The transformation that took place literally gave me an understanding of all the cooperative components of my life. In that moment I experienced and understood at the same time my creative ability as my higher self. I refer to this as the godlike branch of pure consciousness, manifested from nonphysical awareness into the physical, material world.

In theory, we understand the aha moments of life as an expansion of perception, which then alters our future. The ripple effect experience that I encountered allowed all the cooperative components across my lifetime, from my date of birth to the collective present awareness at that time, to merge. All my knowledge, understanding, and past experiences collided, and the resulting ripple effect changed my history and future. It is unclear to me if this altered the collective experience in a sizable way, but I have personally observed its effects on immediate family members living in close proximity to me. I believe the change or shift of that very moment transformed me and my existence. I have contemplated that very event and mapped out the process and cooperative components in as much detail as I could many times in an effort to understand it further. I believe with a good understanding, the process may be evaluated and repeated so that others may experience and understand a similar transformative event within their life experience. Exciting, emotional, heightened awareness, being awestruck … expressing the emotions and intensity of the event.

The belief and understanding that we can change our future is a well-accepted belief. Through processes and information, human beings are able to perceive opportunities and make decisions that affect the direction of their lives. This essentially alters the mindset of the individual, which is then used to create desired future experiences and manifestations. When the cooperative components are identified and understood, it becomes a repeatable process. On a collective level, I believe Jesus's death, burial, and resurrection experience provided a transformative event that rippled across the collective past, present, and future time/space reality. All possibilities. This can even be viewed as forgiveness or salvation from a believer's perspective. It is my perception that all the cooperative components throughout the life of Jesus were identified and evaluated during the Garden of Gethsemane experience, including the upcoming event of the physical trauma experience, including acceptance of the past, present, and future events. This also fulfilled his life purpose, creating a ripple effect that altered the past, present, and future. I would imagine that time may have stood still during this transformative event. It is not my desire or intent to compare my personal ripple effect event to that of the recorded biblical Jesus. However, it is the only conceptual example that I know to use to demonstrate the ripple effect as a miraculous transformation. It also accounts for the multiple, consistent accounts of the events leading up to the death, burial, and recorded resurrection from the followers and believers at that time. The implications of the ripple effect allow an understanding for all possibilities. "With God all things are possible" (Matthew 19:26 NIV).

On the day of this event, I was attempting to organize all the physical objects, pictures, memories, albums, notes, and journals of my life into six separate tote bags. My intention was to separate all of these experiences and memories, including pictures and mementos, into personal life segments. I had acquired six totes, one for each group, to be placed in storage for review at a later time. My intentions were to store all my keepsakes so that I could retrieve any of the totes to jar my memory for a future book or blog post of that certain time period. I labeled the six segments of my life based on monumental events or decisions that took place during that time frame. The first included my birth to age seventeen. The second tote was labeled age eighteen through pregnancy of first child. The third tote was labeled age twenty through pregnancy of second child. The fourth tote was labeled age twenty-six through pregnancy of third child. The fifth tote was labeled age twenty-eight through graduation from college. And the sixth tote was labeled age thirty through graduation of postgraduate degree program. This sixth tote included the segment for passing the family nurse practitioner board exam and beginning career endeavors on a full-time level while continuing the calling of motherhood at a full-time level.

Additional components emerged as I listed contents to be included within each tote: two marriages, multiple family pets, various productive activities involving each child as well as the whole family, and various employment positions, as well as divine interventions and various losses and gains. This included my various living environments, from apartment to mobile home to a regular house and my dream home with a beautiful view. Every component listed demonstrated a significant positive or negative energy. I guess you could call it good and bad events. Positive and negative.

During the process of reliving each cooperative component as a memory and feeling the associated emotion with each memory, I started to notice a pattern emerge around each memory. As this pattern lit up in my mind, I experienced it as a visual stimulus. It was as clear as a table or lamp sitting in front of me. The visual that I was receiving was not material and would not have been visible for anyone else to see outwardly. However, it was very present within my conscious awareness. The images that I was receiving separated themselves into two categories. I labeled them positive and negative events, experiences, and emotions. Categorizing and labeling is nothing new for me. I have done this since I was a child. I have organized things in groups, whether it be by alphabetical order or by color or by size, since I was old enough to do so. Organizing and labeling things has always helped me to feel clear and able to move forward in areas of my life that begin to get uncomfortable. So it is no wonder that my mind has developed the ability to do what I've always done, just on a much larger, nonphysical basis. I was very intrigued by the categories and organization that was going on within my mind, and I continued through segments four and five, and the life experiences and memories continued to repeat the patterns of positive and negative categories. It was like a jigsaw puzzle coming into focus. It was a mind-blowing experience at this time of pattern recognition.

My clarity continued to gain momentum as the focus accumulated more puzzle pieces until a term affiliated with the teachings of Abraham Hicks presented itself in a full understanding of its meaning within my mind. Cooperative components. I said *awe* out loud as well as within my mind. The pattern of emerging positive and negative life experiences and events, including all the physical participants, were the collective cooperating components that made up my entire physical existence. I sat in that thought in that moment for an unknown amount of time. I was not aware of my surroundings as I am writing this chapter right now. I was digitally experiencing all the experiences, events, emotions, and components across my memory and life span. And then it happened. A connection was formed as the puzzle pieces or cooperative components entangled like a spiderweb. Each of these components was interlocked up, down, left, and right. Every direction. Like a configuration of neurons mapping out a new pathway, but this map involved the collection of my entire life memories, experiences, events, emotions, people, locations, animals, feelings, books, desires, fears, and rejections, including all physical and material manifestations. A knowing followed that concluded these were all the cooperative components of my life. No segment or tote categories remained. All the positive and negative energies affiliated with these categories dissipated, and all the components lost any negative charge or vibration. At that moment my consciousness was exposed to the perfection of every single component of my life and the necessary part that it played in my overall experience. I understood that everything happened at the exact time for the exact reason that would make this very moment the transformative experience that I needed.

All the components of the past were cleared of any negative energy, and all became neutral or positive memories. I had an overwhelming understanding of how each component played an integral part as a necessary component for every event and experience to happen just the way that it did. The transformation took place immediately. The ripple was felt, experienced, and understood throughout my past, present, and future. I cried. I swallowed multiple times. I sat down only to get up and walk around the room multiple times. I felt almost euphoric. A real-life matrix experience had happened, and the implications of the experience were unclear at that moment. My time perception was altered, and I felt a close connection with source.

The conversations that followed later that day demonstrated that not only did I experience this amazing transformation within myself; I noticed the conversations and clarity with others throughout the day followed a similar path. Later that day I received a text that read: "Mom, you are pure positive energy. Never experienced such energy and freedom before in my life. Thank you." That experience and ripple effect was not only beneficial for me but for those who came in contact with me throughout the day. Another conversation took place that day with one of my friends. "Today was an amazing day. Everything flowed so easily, and my decisions were thoughtless and on point. The day flowed so easily that I felt bored even though I got more done today and made multiple important decisions with no effort. It was crazy."

I smiled. I knew that my alignment with source during my contemplation of all the cooperative components of my life provided the understanding that initiated the transformational event.

The beautiful awareness that there are no wrong past decisions, no failures, no bad mistakes, no sins to be punished for, literally changed the vibrational content of my past. I literally felt an energetic and vibrational change of my past. I felt the destruction and breakdown of a significant amount of guilt, negative energy, anger, sadness, and negative emotions. I guess you could say they were forgiven, and some were forgotten, to be remembered no more. Alignment with source can occur unconsciously as well as consciously. Intentional alignment with source occurs when thoughts produce manifestations within the mind that become cooperative components. In other words, when we think thoughts that align with our inner source, we align with pure positive energy. Pure love. Transformations take place, and our perception enlarges to that of our inner source at that moment. Wholeness and total satisfaction was the end result.

The revelation of that event constructed the following understanding and revealed the creator and the creation as one. At the core of awareness, I was there. I was the same being that I am now, only more. The cooperative components of my past were my own unconscious manifestations that became the cooperative components to my own evolution and expansion. I had the ability to create perfect life experiences before I even knew what I needed to grow and expand. How awesome it is to know that there is a creative force within our world, within each individual being, that we can trust and know and depend on. It knows each one of us on a very personal basis, and we have access to its intelligence and creative ability at will. We are so powerful and free to choose that we can choose bondage. We can also choose love and trust and power in the knowing that we are not alone and inside every one of us lies a powerful, creative force patiently waiting for our attention and desire to connect with it. Ever present. All powerful. Pure positive energy flowing directly to us at all times. All we must do is align with it and allow it to flow to us and through us. Now that is pure genius!

CHAPTER 10

SELF-AWARENESS

Dr. Joe Dispenza said, "Thoughts are the language of the brain and feelings are the language of the body." A belief is only a thought you keep thinking and feeling over and over. Like the unfolding art of a flower and the geometric shapes and designs of the mandala, the mind, body, and soul experience a repeating pattern of the spiritual experience. This same pattern can be seen throughout the cosmos, in a spiral seashell, a pine cone, a dandelion, and the perpetual shape and dimension within a honeycomb. This precise, consistent design throughout all of nature is also demonstrated throughout the consciousness arising within evolved human beings.

The act of looking for something automatically creates a new something to see. Look for greatness. Look for beauty. Look for good. Look for kindness. Self-awareness could be considered consciousness observing itself in the physical realm. The state of consciousness or state of being leads to the outward unfolding from an inward motion, moving forward through expansion. This helix pattern design unfolds consistently as Mother Earth, a conscious being, throughout nature and emerges as plant life, animal life, and human life manifestations. This repetitive cycle can be visibly seen as the 7 billion manifestations, all appearing as individual creations yet collectively making up the whole. The seasons, the phases of the moon, the tides of the ocean, the hibernation of bears, the flight pattern of birds—all of it demonstrates the art of conscious creation.

Self-awareness is our ability to view our own personal reality and create from that awareness. We are creating all the time. Whether it is conscious creation or unconscious creation, we are creating our own reality nonetheless. Once we grasp the concept that we are creating our own life experience, we can then make a conscious effort to learn and understand how we can deliberately create what we want in our reality. All that we can experience with our senses was once a thought, focused on and then manifested into this dimension. The beauty and brilliance of this natural world was once a vibrational thought. High-rise condominiums, microchip software programs, MRI technology, Apple iPhones, GPS navigational software, astronomical satellites, and next-day delivery from Amazon were all merely a thought or idea at one point in time.

So much of this modern world's creations was unconsciously created. By unconscious creation, I mean the thought was received and the idea germinated in the mind of an individual who then acted in response to the thought by desire. Regardless of the reason or motivation of the actions, the desire to see the idea manifest is what brought it into fruition. With this understanding from a consciously aware, intentional mind, I wonder why we, as human beings, are not creating at a rapid speed all the futuristic technologies we long to see manifested. There must be more to it than just the process or formula of creation. On a grand scale then, life is essentially the unfolding pattern of growth, demonstrated as all that is, into the manifested physical realm that we are currently experiencing. The depth and continual unfolding become so intense and heavy on a thought level that description becomes difficult and challenging. However, just like the daily consistent rising sun, the day is followed by the nighttime moon and its consistent moon phases, which are repeated every day and every night.

Vibrational alignment then is demonstrated as the unfolding expansion of source consciousness into our physical reality. From unconscious to conscious. From thought to reaction. From thought to intentional action. To another thought to conscious action to then conscious thought, conscious action, and so on. With the awareness of self comes the identification of life's cooperative components and the processes that produce further unfolding of this life experience. All of this is now shifting from an unconscious creation perspective to a conscious creation perspective. The capabilities of the human mind, with focused attention, have revealed patterns of thought and behaviors that produce very consistent results. With the analysis of these events, patterns, and experiences comes an understanding of the expansion of life as we know it. Just like any other process, conscious creation—or unconscious creation for that matter—can be broken down and repeated.

All things are energy. Energy is particles or material in action or vibration. Patterns of vibration or levels of vibration make up our material world, and consciousness experiences the material world through each and every one of its conscious beings. Pure positive energy or source or God is the creator and also the one who experiences the creation. "But with God all things are possible" (Matthew 19:26 NIV) makes a lot of sense with the understanding of who and what we are. Limitless possibilities.

With this new understanding, so many things make sense now. Over the past twenty years, I have spent many hours thinking about and planning my future. I never quite knew how it worked, but I quickly saw that when I made a list of things to do each day or things that I wanted to accomplish throughout the year, they always seemed to get done. When I merely thought about things that I needed to do or wanted to do but I did not write them down, they did not always materialize. Because I have always done a substantial amount of thinking throughout the day, I just developed the habit of writing things down and checking them off as I got them done. This is definitely a part of the creation process. The thought is received, written down, reviewed, and fulfilled. The following are from my personal journals at various stages of adulthood. They provide a basis for the creation process that has helped me understand and repeat desired results.

Journal Entry

The person I am (becoming)

I get up in the morning at 6:00 a.m. feeling refreshed and rejuvenated. I stretch or do yoga for ten to twenty minutes each day. I let my dog out. I wake my boys up, and we spend time together before we start the day. I put on a beautiful feminine dress outfit with coordinating jewelry and high-heeled shoes. Which I love. I put my makeup on, and I fix my beautiful long hair. Everyone compliments my hair and my style. I take my Kyani and travel to work, feeling great.

I treat all people with respect and compassion. I am mindful and intentional. I am authentic and well-liked. I am desired. I have attractive feminine character. Integrity, honesty, kindness are just my nature. I am an author. I love my career, and I make a lot of money. I just sold my book for $1 million. I am very beautiful and confident. I am kind and genuine, and I see miracles every day. My patients love me. I come in to visit them, and I listen to each patient and family member as they share their reality. I am an inspiration. I am wise.

Journal Entry

I am falling in love with a man who desires a spiritual journey and loves dogs. We meditate and pray together. I respect him and love looking at him. I can feel his genuine, kind masculinity when he enters a room, and I desire him. I desire to be his wife. I desire to please him and love him. I am his, and he is mine. He loves my mind and talks deeply with me about consciousness. He is my best friend. He is authentic, trustworthy, and outdoorsy, with a rough exterior. He loves to share his insight and experiences with me. He and I both share the same goal: to add value to each other's lives as well as those we come in contact with. He is a man of character. We grow together. We love to be with each other. He thinks I am brilliant and beautiful. He loves me for me. And I love him for his beingness.

Journal Entry

Long-Range Goals: Be debt-free, student loans and home paid for. Close relationships. Travel. Sightsee. Watch my children grow. Take my dogs places. Be on time. Work effectively and creatively. Impact my patients and my coworkers. Continually improve my character.

Journal Entry

Daily rituals: meditation, contemplation, appreciation one hour

Water/Fuel/Exercise

Continual learning (audios, documentaries)

Four-hour workday (two hours housework, two hours focused on book)

Spend time with MK, my boys, dogs, and family.

✳ ✺ ✢ ✷

Latest Journal Entry

I am connected to source. Source is always present and flowing to me. Life is always working out for me through the path of least resistance. False premise beliefs are dissolving one by one, and my thoughts, words, and actions are in alignment. I am fully abundant, and I am allowing more and more abundance into my reality every day.

I am always aware of my feelings and make a conscious effort to understand them. Anytime I do not feel good, I am not aligned with source. It is *not* anything or anyone apart from me causing my discomfort (anger, fear, jealousy, confusion). It is only a separation of alignment from my source.

I speak to myself and others with gratitude, kindness, honesty, and appreciation. I no longer look at what is because I know that current reality is an old manifestation. I do appreciate all the valuable experiences in the life lessons I have learned. My boys provide me with daily reminders of my positive traits and seeker mentality just by watching their life. I value myself, this beautiful vibrational life, and all who cross my path.

The thoughts and words that we use on a daily basis are words of creation. If we consciously consider the truth and validity that our thoughts and words create our reality, we will pay close attention to what we think and say. We will also become very attentive to the words, images, movies, and environments that we allow our senses to experience. The law of attraction provides a consistent receiving comparable to the vibration that we emit. For this reason, it is understandable that we are very similar to our environment. If we consistently have the same thoughts, we consistently create similar experiences over and over. If you are not happy with the life that you are creating and living, then change it. Change your daily thought patterns. This can be done with small daily processes that interrupt the patterns that hold you hostage in your current reality. Just the fact that you are reading this book demonstrates the ability to make small adjustments in your daily routine.

Through self-awareness, we are able to see our own reality, our own vibration. How you feel at any given time throughout the day is an indicator of your level of vibration. The highest level of vibration experience is freedom, love, empowerment, appreciation, and joy. We have all felt these feelings, and ultimately they are what we are after. Every goal, every endeavor, every desire, all have the same desired end result of feeling good or better than we currently do. If we can adjust our vibration without accomplishing a desired goal or endeavor, any and every experience becomes an awesome experience that leads to an awesome life.

My daily routine starts with an hour of meditation, contemplation, and appreciation. Water is essential as well. These are nonnegotiable. Daily alignment is my purpose. Everything I say or think or do is enhanced in a way that makes a remarkable difference every day from an aligned state of being.

My desires in life have remained the same as long as I can remember. Inner and outer beauty/attractiveness, beautiful, feminine clothing, classy behavior, kind, giving, loving personality, and authentic, genuine character. As I started seeking clarity of purpose and direction in my life throughout my thirties, I discovered my desires remained; however, the recipients changed. The more aligned I get, the less I can tolerate people and lower vibrational beings. All the negative, off feelings that I previously overlooked or buried around certain people amplified and just simply became unacceptable. No more showing up to reunions or birthday parties that my inner GPS indicate will ruin my vibe. However, I am developing the ability to maintain my high feeling vibration even in the presence of people who previously caused me to disconnect with source. I realize that the memories of the past are primarily responsible for this dip or wobble, so I am just very selective in my attention now. This transition has not been an easy one. I have struggled on multiple occasions with internal conflict surrounding the feelings and thoughts that I have experienced. I am realizing that my programming is deeply ingrained within my subconscious and does not dissipate just because I have chosen to eliminate negativity from my reality. It is a process. A daily battle at times. But every day the momentum of my new alignment gains energy, and when I am truly aligned, there is no feeling like it. The experience of alignment is a mix of falling in love, a drug-like euphoria, and laser focus all bundled up in one experience. I believe it is the most powerful force on this planet. It is pure positive energy. It is *love*. It offers forgiveness as far as the east is from the west. It remembers offenses no more. It looks through my eyes as if a child were seeing an ocean or wild animal for the first time every time. It is playful and curious. It has access to all-knowing intelligence and can flow with music like a magic-carpet ride. Heaven on earth. Priceless. Unshakable. Irrefutable. Fairy tale–like. Freedom, joy, appreciation, and love for self and others. Once the feeling of alignment has been experienced, it cannot be forgotten. Nothing else will do. Wars and suffering and ill treatment cannot exist in its pure-form presence. Darkness is cast out when resistance within dissolves. Alignment is the awakening, the second coming, the new heaven and new earth. It is the drug addict's high and the middle class workers' Friday paycheck. It is the weight lifter entering the zone and the runner's high. It is *being* in the flow.

CHAPTER 11

THE POWER OF COCREATION

Nikola Tesla said, "If you want to find the secrets of the universe, think in terms of energy, frequency, and vibration." Formulas and numbers play an important part in understanding creation. For this book I have included some various numbers, including ratios and percentages, that I use in my daily life. All have significant meaning to me as an individual and may or may not resonate with you.

I am including similarities that I use to demonstrate my understanding of the creation process. The ability to create a business or chart-topping song has been sought after for generations and continues to evolve. However, my description of the individual creation process is not new or mine to claim. Albert Einstein's $E = MC^2$ demonstrates the creation process from nonphysical to the material world that we experience. Energy or consciousness is produced or the action result of source (pure positive energy/God) in nonphysical form. Pure positive energy or source is then the totality of pure masculine energy and pure feminine energy multiplied by itself. Being x doing equals source or pure energy.

This may be difficult to visualize and understand, but there is clearly a relationship between the masculine and feminine energy, including the magnetic attraction. This does not entirely mean male and female. It represents the masculine qualities of logic, action, and reasoning, as previously discussed in part I of this book, as well as the feminine qualities of creativity, compassion, and community. One could say that a vibrationally aligned human being has both feminine and masculine energies, favorably merging the action, logic, and reasoning with the feminine quality of being and compassion into a whole being. My interpretation of God consciousness/source/ pure positive energy from the nonphysical into the material, space-time reality resulted in a whole human being or the masculine and feminine being, for example, Adam and Eve as separate individuals or one individual expressing both masculine and feminine energies.

The current shift in energies around the planet leads me to believe that people are awakening to a new understanding of what wholeness really means. For me, I am finding an inner awareness that wholeness is possible when I am vibrationally aligned with source. We all have access to our higher self when resistance diminishes or is released within the mind. Esther Hicks has produced an array of processes and books outlining the teachings of Abraham. Included are techniques to achieve alignment with our higher self or source. These processes help to achieve higher vibration in the now when put into practice. I have used these processes to reach alignment as well as to develop my own personal daily processes or formulas to fit my lifestyle.

The following formulas or ratios are part of my creative process. 6:1. Six days of purposeful daily routine and one day unplanned. 3:1. Daily care of my mind, body, and spirit. 2:1. Cocreation between myself and my higher self, which I refer to as source, in addition to cocreation between myself and my current life partner. There is power in the presence of two like-minded individuals with complementing energies of alignment. Source knows all there is, and when I attain alignment with source, I receive vibrations or thoughts that I am able to understand and decipher at a level that is not attainable from lower vibration states. Likewise, when I communicate with my partner my thoughts and desires from this aligned state, we vibrationally align and complement each other's understanding through resonance. This is difficult to describe and is not always possible during every encounter. However, if you have experienced this mind alignment with another individual, you will *know* what I am attempting to describe. Time stands still or feels completely altered. Focused attention becomes a flow-like state, and amazing ideas and connections erupt simultaneously. I have also experienced this same cocreation flow while listening to audios and YouTube videos of valuable visionaries, as if we were both physically present. Quantum physics is on the curb of understanding and describing such unexplainable occurrences. What a wonderful time to be alive in this modern time-space reality!

As I mentioned above, a formula for creation was previously presented to the world and scientific community by Albert Einstein, I have also identified a percentage of masculine and feminine energies as I understand and perceive them. I call it the 80/20. I am noticing in my personal reality as well as the shift that is universally taking place a significant shift from *doing* to *being*. The masculine action-oriented quality to a more feminine being-oriented quality. In my own personal life, I have greatly reduced the daily action-oriented habits and behaviors that I lived the majority of my life. As I became more consistent with my daily desire to align with source, I started losing interest in a lot of activities that I did on a daily basis. This was a rough transition to make for me and my family. My career life changed significantly, as well as my desire for entertainment. My mind and spirit became my primary focus, and my physical well-being became streamlined. Self-care has become a high priority, as well as my daily meditation, contemplation, and appreciation processes. I changed my daily action-oriented tasks to 20 percent of my day, including both career and home care maintenance. Four hours per day. Total. Which leaves me with twenty hours to sleep, play, dream, spend time on the water and at the movies, and most importantly self-care (which includes trips to Ulta). My twenty hours of each day are now my *being* hours. The remaining four hours are focused on my purpose/contribution/career and home. All of these life changes evolved out of my desire for authenticity and alignment. The emotions and feelings experienced throughout the changes that have taken place have been from one end of the stick to the other. Fun, empowerment, freedom, and bliss on one end and fatigue, depression, and overwhelm on the other. A better description would be like a boulder rolling off a hill that reaches the bottom and finds a resting place. The momentum of the fast, action-oriented life slowed to a stop, and my understanding and acceptance of the changes taking place took on the intensity of all emotions experienced. Eventually, the boulder of momentum started back up the new way of living, and the vibration quickly elevated on a more consistent level. I understand this experience as growth and expansion. There have been days that I found getting out of bed to be too much activity. Understanding the changes in my physical body from the changes in vibrational alignment has been quite a wild ride. I stand in awe and appreciation for the experiences, the understandings, the connections, and the shifts in my conscious awareness and ability to communicate these experiences. It is my desire that my journey will resonate with others experiencing the same growth, and together we will expand our creative abilities to achieve the highest vibrational level across all continents. The possibilities are endless and exciting.

The creation process can be demonstrated in different ways, as well as from an individual and collective perspective. Esther Hicks identifies five steps of creation in her book, Ask and It Shall Be Given, essentially as Ask-step I, Source Answers-Step II, Receive or Allow-Step III, Get really good at step 3-Step IV and Growth through Contrast- Step-V.

The five stages of creation and receiving on a collective level from my perspective are outlined below.

1. Nonphysical consciousness to material world/sensory only perception (source to masculine and feminine physical presence).

2. Material/sensory perception to habits/beliefs/instinctual human behavior (human beings to human doings).

3. Instinctual, habitual human behavior to contrasting self-destruction and self-preservation behavior.

4. Self-awareness of self-destructing behavior versus self-preserving behavior to intentional, conscious knowledge

and understanding of self-preservation (including the earth and all inhabitants, creatures, and living parts).

5. Self-actualization. understanding of self, internal GPS and time/space reality, cooperative components, contrast, desire, creation ability/formula, cocreation and alignment. as generational healing potential.

Individual alignment allows for universal growth and expansion. Each and every one of us is a part of this unfolding. Creation is constantly taking place with or without our conscious participation. However, conscious creation is gaining momentum globally, and the shift is steadily impacting all humanity. For years I have absorbed all possible knowledge and information, including various perspectives from the most influential creators on the planet. Seekers and visionaries, artists and performers. Inspirational influencers like Tony Robbins, Leonardo DiCaprio, and Jason Silva; musical performers like Post Malone, Ava Max, and Billie Eilish; social media platforms like Instagram and Twitter; and one-name historical figures Jesus, Einstein, and Aristotle continue to be quoted and respected. All have left a permanent fingerprint on humanity, and their cocreation with source cannot be denied. Joseph Campbell coined the root of alignment when he suggested for his students to "Follow your bliss," which will put you back on a path that has always been there just waiting for you.

CHAPTER 12

TRANSFORMATION
THROUGH CONTRAST

We have all experienced *aha* moments in life. When a concept is planted within the mind, intellectual understanding usually occurs. But if you understand and experience all of the components involved in the concept, a connection can be made and felt. I call these moments *aha* moments. For example, if you see and hear all the advertised benefits of yoga and read all the scientific research that adds the factual observed data, suggesting repeatable results, you may believe and understand that yoga is good and has beneficial side effects. However, until you experience the actual physical, spiritual, and emotional effects of yoga, you will not be transformed by the experience with a knowing or full understanding. We experience these types of events throughout our lifetime, and we advance in understanding, and occasionally we are transformed by the event. I have personally experienced so many aha moments that I can say knowledge and information that resonate with me, causing an aha moment, are my favorite high. Once I realized that it was more than just listening to audios and seminars and reading books that I enjoyed, that it was the neural connections taking place in my brain, I set out to discover this thrill in my life on a daily basis.

Not only do I love the chemicals produced in my brain by the connections and new neural pathways produced during these euphoric moments; I now understand that this is also the path to growth and expansion on both a personal and collective level. I have experienced some events in my life that have brought me to my knees, that have transformed the entire direction of my life and brought me to the timely conclusion that the human experience is nothing short of miraculous. Writing this book has not been an option for me. Source has led and on some occasions dragged me to a place in my life where this was the next and only step. As I become more whole within myself, I am merging the masculine and feminine energies in an aligned way that my individual being came here to be, do, and experience. I realize that within the masculine energies of logic, reasoning, and action, I am able to follow my inner guidance through inspired action. My feminine energies of creativity, compassion, and gentleness are allowing me to identify my core desired feelings by giving attention to not only my desires but both positive and negative life experiences. Once I make some sense of how all life experiences are beneficial and necessary, I can then place my focus on the desired experiences that build positive momentum within me. In other words, I am the center of my own world as well as the creator. This may appear very selfish, but once you experience the aligned connection with source and you realize that your thoughts are the only resistance cutting off that alignment, you and your thoughts become your focus.

Come with me as we travel back in time to a moment that began a series of events that changed the direction of my life in 2010. The secretary at the office that I was working in as a nurse practitioner called for me over the intercom to let me know I had a personal phone call at the desk. I made my way to the desk and picked up the phone, and I could feel the fear in the voice on the other end of the phone. I remember hearing the words, "Sarah, your dad has fallen off a two-story house from the roof. The ambulance is on its way, and a helicopter has been called to help with transport to a trauma hospital." My knees buckled, and I gasped for the next breath. I knew in that moment that this was extremely serious. I don't know how I knew, but I had a knowing.

I gathered myself back together just like I always could, adjusted my professional demeanor, and made the decision that I would see the four patients who had already been taken back to the exam rooms. The staff would need to reschedule and redirect all the remaining patients who were scheduled for that day. I walked in to see the next patient. With my heart thumping in my throat, I asked them, "What brings you here today?" I don't remember the outcome of patients one, two, or three. I only vaguely remember even walking from room to room during that time. But I remember the fourth patient. I walked into the room, sat down beside the patient, and turned to my computer to begin typing the patient's complaint; and before I had the chance to ask what problems she was experiencing, she blurted out, "It's about time you finally got in here."

The racing heartbeat in my chest paused for just a second as I lifted my head up from my computer. I turned slightly, looked her dead in the eyes, and spoke in a very professional, kind manner. "I apologize for your wait today. I also want you to know that I have a family emergency going on as we speak. My dad has fallen off a roof that he was working on at a two-story home, and he is lying on the ground waiting for a helicopter to pick him up. I do not know the severity of it, but I do know it's an emergent situation. I chose to see all my patients who had already been brought back to the patient rooms before I leave, and you are my last patient. Please tell me what has brought you in today so that I can help you before I leave to go check on my dad."

The lady's jaw dropped open, and I saw her take a long, deep breath. She looked me right in the eyes and said with a very genuine, compassionate tone, "I am so sorry. I shouldn't have complained, and I haven't been waiting very long. I'm sorry to hear about your dad."

The next ten to fifteen minutes are a blur to me, but at some point, I finished seeing that patient, finished the necessary documentation and orders, gathered my things from my office, walked out, and got in my vehicle. I drove rather calmly with a sick feeling in my stomach about an hour and a half to the hospital where he was taken. I got out of the car, walked into the hospital, and was led back to an exam room where my dad was. His brother Tim was standing at the entrance of the very open trauma room with his hands in both of his front pockets. I looked him in the eyes as I came down the hallway and turned to walk into the room.

There lay my dad on a stretcher. He had chest tubes in both lungs, and he was moaning under his breath.

I walked over to the head of the stretcher, and I said, "I love you, Dad." Time stood still for a minute or five, I'm not sure which. The doctors and nurses were coming in and out of the room talking among themselves.

The only thing I remember my dad saying to me was, "Go on out of here; I don't want you to see me like this."

I remember backing up across the room and in a low, rebellious voice said, "I'm not going anywhere."

My uncle came over and stood beside me. In a whisper he said, "Don't cry; that will upset him, and he doesn't need that right now."

I knew that was true. So that's what I did. I just took it all in. In a very short period of time, the emergency room staff had him stable enough to be transferred to a university hospital with an experienced trauma team due to his extensive injuries. So the helicopter crew loaded him on board the helicopter, and I made arrangements for my kids to be picked up from school that day and headed toward the university hospital. I arrived at the hospital a couple hours later and found my dad in the emergency room. He was still lying on the same stretcher in a much smaller room with a lot less activity going on in the room and hallways. My dad's wife and I waited for the doctor to come around to get an update. Dad was far from comfortable but was no longer moaning or grimacing in pain.

The doctor came in and explained all the fractures and injuries and then directed the focus toward the injuries that needed priority attention and intervention. He had five broken vertebrae in his back; one of those five was a burst fracture, which essentially means the bone was shattered and fragmented or displaced. He had nine fractured ribs. One of them was completely displaced from its origin. His scapula bone was fractured, along with his sternum or what some call the breastplate. Doctors reported that they did not feel that there was any brain involvement from the traumatic fall, which was good news. The chest tubes were keeping the lungs inflated, which were both injured from the impact of the fall. The next couple of days were emotional ups and downs, not knowing what the outcome would be, but there was a level of relief just in the fact that he had survived the accident.

The priority was the spine. There was a trauma team and also a spinal orthopedic team monitoring the progress. After two or three days, the two teams were not completely in agreement on the treatment regimen. The orthopedic spinal team suggested that surgical intervention was necessary and the best course of action. The trauma providers suggested a brace to stabilize the spine. So a brace was ordered specifically for his body dimensions and was placed on him. On about the fourth day, the trauma team decided that they wanted to stand him up to see if he could walk. His wife and I, as well as the spinal orthopedic team, were very uneasy about this decision; however, attempts were made to get him from a lying position to a sitting position and then to a standing position. This process took ten to fifteen minutes, and as his feet made contact with the floor, I heard him mumble a desperate plea for them to stop. They proceeded on, and as they started to lift him into a standing position, he yelled out, turned three different shades of gray, and blacked out. So I'm sure you can imagine the next course of action, which was surgery.

They took him to surgery and installed two titanium rods down the majority of the length of his spine and attached them with nuts and bolts and screws. They returned him back from surgery on a ventilator, where he remained alert and awake throughout the whole day while he was still intubated.

I remember being in the room standing right beside the bed as he started waking up from surgery, and panic instilled within him as he woke up with the tube down his throat breathing for him. His hands were softly cuffed to the sides of the bed so that he would not pull the tube out as he began to wake up. I remember him looking at me and mouthing the words, "Help me." As I saw his panic amplify, the panic within me started to amplify, and I asked the doctors to please help him or knock him out. They explained to me that due to the nature of his injuries and the surgical intervention that it was important that they keep him awake so that they would know if there was any neurological impairment or feeling loss of his legs as the day went by. The next couple of days, my dad showed a lot of improvement and was sitting up with assistance by day six. It seemed like we were finally on the path to recovery. The human body and spirit can absorb more than most can imagine.

One week had passed, and I was exhausted. Dad was finally moved from the trauma unit to a step-down care unit at the university. This room was a little more private, and a few family members continued to take turns staying in the room to help with his care. That night my dad's sister and I were in the room. My aunt was semi-reclined in the window opening, and I was in the only chair in the room. It was about four o'clock in the morning when I noticed the vibration of my cell phone. My ringer was off. I sluggishly picked up my phone and answered the call. It was my mother.

For a moment the entire world and time stopped as I listened to her shaking voice tell me the news. "Sarah, your brother has been in a car accident, and he is being airlifted to the closest hospital as we speak."

I felt as if I was dreaming. I literally felt that this was impossible to happen at the same time that Dad was hospitalized. It took me a moment to come to the realization that I was actually awake. So like I always did, I gathered my adult face and composure and got up to gather my suitcase to leave. I attempted to leave as quietly as I could, but as I walked out of the hospital room, Dad spoke up. "What's wrong?" I calmly told him that Mom had called and that Les was in a car accident and on his way to the hospital. "I don't know much about what is going on, but I'm going to drive to the hospital and meet Mom. I'll let you know something soon."

I drove for a few hours although it seemed much closer. My focus on the task at hand had me zoned in and undistracted. As I pulled into the hospital parking building in Virginia, I noticed that my mother was in the car in front of me arriving at the same time. We got out of our cars and walked to the entrance of the hospital, where we were greeted by a solemn yet friendly gentleman.

The man, who appeared to be waiting on us at the entrance, was most likely a spokesman for the hospital or had something to do with the business department, as he was dressed in nice slacks, shoes, and a button-up shirt. He was cordial yet direct. He asked if we were the Spencer family, and we both said yes. He then asked, "What do you know about the accident?"

My mother responded, "We don't know anything other than there was a wreck and he was airlifted here."

The gentleman spoke with authority yet compassion. "Mr. Spencer has a catastrophic head injury from the accident. He is currently in surgery to stabilize him. The emergency room physicians had to make the decision to send him to the operating room based on the severity of his injuries as there was no family at the hospital yet to discuss the options with." The gentleman asked if we had any questions. and we just nodded no. He led us to the nearest elevator. and we rode up many floors in silence. Upon arriving at the ninth floor. we walked down a long corridor until we came to a section of the hospital that required authorization to enter.

As we stood at the door awaiting the buzzer to allow us entrance. the gentleman said to my mother, "Your son has survived surgery; however he was given a significant amount of blood products, and they removed his spleen. They fixed his left arm, which originally appeared to be fractured, but upon closer observation in the operating room, it only needed alignment back to its original position. He is on a ventilator, and he is not alert from the operation and medications. I want you to be aware of everything that we know before you walk in the room. The OR surgeon had to remove a large portion of his skull to relieve the pressure from the brain injury. The skin was then placed back where it was to begin with and stapled. There is a significant amount of swelling throughout the whole brain, and we are monitoring the internal pressures as well as the brain stem for herniation. Again, Mr. Spencer has sustained a catastrophic head injury, but we will be monitoring him closely for changes in his condition."

The door opened. A few other family members had arrived by that time, and we all entered the trauma unit on the ninth floor together. As I walked down the hallway toward his room, I noticed that all of the patient trauma rooms had glass doors and walls toward the nurses' desk. As we approached the nurses' desk, they pointed into the room where he was. I remember taking a deep, deep breath as I gathered myself internally to assess the situation.

I walked into the room and saw my brother lying there with a machine breathing for him and what appeared to be a lifeless body. His face was swollen. His head was swollen. He had two black eyes. There were small amounts of dried blood above his ear and down his cheek on the right side. His left arm was wrapped from elbow to fingers and in a sling around his neck. I remember thinking that it looked like they had stuffed him into the bed from head to toe because the soles of his feet were firmly up against the footboard of the bed. I understood because he was six feet five inches tall. No words can describe my thoughts at that moment because I had no thoughts. No words, only absent words. Maybe just blankness or emptiness.

I am not sure how long we all stood there, speechless, before we lifted our heads up and began to look at each other. For a moment it was as if the reality of the situation was just starting to sink in for all who were in the room at the exact same time. It was heavy. It was so heavy in my chest and my throat and on my shoulders.

For the next couple of hours, the nurse who was primarily in charge of his care attempted to update us and keep us aware of all that was going on. She requested that any visitors keep their tones very low, if not silent, to decrease any stimulation that would cause his brain to get excited and cause further damage. She explained that the next twenty-four to forty-eight hours were crucial for him in that the least amount of stimulation, the better his chances of survival were. They kept the room very dark. The window curtains were closed. Aside from the beeping of the equipment and monitors, there was very little sound in the room. She explained that there was a sensor on top of his head that we could see taped over; it was through the skin and planted into a portion of the brain to give pressure readings on how his brain was doing. She made it clear that if the pressures got too high for too long that it would cause a herniation of the brain into the spinal cord area, which is not compatible with life. Ultimately the care was focused on keeping the pressures regulated and at a level compatible with life until there was no more swelling. Regardless of the outcome, his injuries were severe, and the likelihood of full recovery was very poor at that point.

The night before the accident, my brother called me while I was sitting in traffic in Virginia. I was mildly stressed when he called, but I took the call and put him on speaker as I drove.

He said, "You know I'm meeting with a judge tomorrow in Arizona, and I'm not sure which suit I should wear. Which one do you think I should wear?"

I replied, "Wear whichever one you think looks the nicest."

He proceeded to tell me he had a navy blue suit and he had a black suit, and he just wasn't sure which one he should wear.

I remember feeling irritated with the compulsive question that I had already answered, and I said yet again, "I would wear my nicest suit if I was you."

He said okay. He then proceeded to ask me how Dad was doing today and if he was improving.

I told him that he was slightly improved but that it was going to be a long road to recovery.

We talked back and forth for a few moments. I remember feeling some agitation and irritation because of all the traffic that I was in, and I just wanted to get off the phone with him. I wish I knew then what I know now. "I'm in the middle of a lot of traffic and I really need to get off the phone, so I'll talk to you later, okay?" Click. I'm not sure if I even said goodbye. That was the last time I ever heard his voice.

I have relived that moment so many times, just wishing that I had said something different. Wishing that I had been more attentive, kinder, or just listened without rushing him off the phone. So many times I've thought how my situation overwhelmed and consumed me so that I couldn't even see that he was calling because he needed me. He needed my advice. Simple advice, yes, but of all the people he could have called, he called me.

I spent the next six days at the hospital with my brother. Many family members and friends came and went, but I couldn't leave. I spent a lot of time with my brother that week. He never spoke a word to me. Never opened his eyes and looked into mine. I know he knew I was there, though. I got the chance to tell him how proud I was of him in so many areas. In fact, I caught up on a lifetime of things I should have said. For once I wasn't in a big rush to go anywhere or be anywhere or get anything done. I sat in a chair beside the bed and took a lot of deep breaths and focused all my attention right then and there on him. I noticed how dark black his hair was that they had not shaved off. And how he had a nose just like my grandmother's. His shoulders were pretty broad, and his legs were so long. I put my hands on his shoulder and upper arm and laid my head on his chest for the first time in my life and hugged him like I would a long-lost friend. Every glance, every touch, every hug was so precious, and I took it all in as if time was standing still just for me.

There were so many moments that stand out during that week as if they were imprinted into my memory with heightened emotion. The organ transplant team met at some point during the week to discuss the options of organ donation and possible recipients. We were advised that my brother had made himself an organ donor a month prior to the accident and that the physicians at the hospital felt that he would not recover and that organ transplantation would follow shortly. Everyone said their goodbyes except for our dad.

The hospital staff made arrangements to have our father transported to the hospital from the hospital he was recovering in. Dad was still unable to stand or roll over in the bed. He was alert but somewhat medicated from all the injuries and back surgery days before. His suffering was one that few can understand. I suffered greatly too. Watching my dad be wheeled up in a hospital bed, with all his injuries, beside his dying son was very difficult to watch. I loved them both so much. I also felt the pain of a parent saying last goodbyes to a son. In all honesty I blocked a lot of my emotions. I had to. There was nowhere left for them to reside. My dad was so broken physically and emotionally, my mom was devastated, and I was the only one capable of staying with my brother until the organ procurement procedure.

The last day I spent with my brother was a heightened experience. It was just me and him. I watched the nurses and doctors carefully monitor his urine output, his cardiac output, his body temperature, and various other parameters. I understood the need to care for the organs that would be placed in another's body to offer them a second chance at living. There were many moments that I did not feel that I was awake. Time was not as I knew it to be. The steady flow of energy and clear minded thoughts confused me. I was at peace with my final week with my brother. I had no regret or desire to change anything about those final days. You could say I had a peace that passeth all understanding. Acceptance that things would never be the same. Acceptance that the past had served its purpose.

As the clock ticked closer to twelve, I gathered all the emotional strength left within me. With his heart beating and all vital signs demonstrating life still present, I wondered if the surgeon would medicate him before opening up his body to retrieve his organs. His room began to fill with nurses and hospital staff as the machines were unhooked and prepared for transport down to surgery. I walked behind them as they ushered him down the hallway into an oversize elevator. At last, the time had come. A moment that I will never forget. The elevator door opened, and a long hallway stood in front of the OR opening. The hospital staff all took multiple steps back away from his bed and told me that this was as far as I could go with him. Ahead was a set of double doors and a surgical team awaiting his appearance. I stood at his side and looked him over. I felt every emotion that I had ever experienced in that moment. I wanted to beg them to give him one more day to move or flinch or show signs of life. I wanted this moment to never end. I leaned over his bed and whispered five little words in his ear as I wrapped my arms as far around him as I could reach. I can still feel those words as they flowed from my lips, but it was not I who flowed those words to him. No. It was God who breathed those words through my lips and into both my brother's ear as well as my own. "I'm so proud of you!"

I refused to walk away. I told the nurse that I would *not* walk away from him, that they would have to take him away from me because I would never walk away and leave someone I loved by choice. She nodded and confidently pulled the side rail back up for transport. Her duty was to transport him with organs viable and intact to the operating room; however, she allowed me to hold on to his hand as she pushed his warm body forward down the hall toward the double doors. The resistance that we both felt as she pushed his bed away from me did not deter her course of action. As I held true to my promise, she slid his hand out of mine and gently placed it back at his side, never missing a step as the remaining medical staff surrounded his bed and continued the solemn escort to fulfill his destiny. May you never stand in that same powerless position. But if you do, surrender.

Over the past nine years, I have pondered on these events as well as many other monumental events that have taken place in my life. I have developed my intuition. I have gained a great deal of knowledge through life experiences, consistent, daily self-education, and internal contemplation and reflection of my life. I would almost consider it an obsession that I have had for as long as I can remember, to find what I was longing for. And what I have discovered is this: Life is about growth and expansion. There is no joy without sadness, no sunshine without rain. With every desire comes a contrasting opposite of that desire. There is wanted and unwanted, and life is the unfolding of desire, contrast, and experience. The physical human body is equipped with a beautifully orchestrated navigating system. When we begin to understand it and experience life from that understanding, the game comes alive with the odds in our favor.

For centuries, human beings have been searching for meaning and discoveries to better understand this planet and themselves. From an instinctual perspective, it makes sense to study the environment, the laws of nature, and attempt to define its boundaries and limits. However, we are waking up. The collective consciousness is teetering as the masses awaken to a deeper understanding and awareness. The unconscious are becoming conscious. We are no longer only aware of the external environment; we are shifting our awareness to the internal environment, which we now know creates our external world. This experience left me changed. The human heart cannot experience the heightened emotions of pain and surrender without transmutation. Unconditional love is transformational.

Through daily meditation, contemplation, and appreciation of all life experiences, I have come to realize that my brother was a key component in my experience. The events that took place during that time period altered my perspective significantly. Life took on a deeper meaning. Living with no regret became my mantra. His sacrifice was my gain. The level of integrity and authenticity within myself became a commitment between me and God. I made the decision that I wanted to tell the people I loved how much I loved them every day. No more wasted days on insignificant tasks. No more showing up to places that I didn't feel called to go. No more watching life pass me by. Every day became a special day. For a long time I demonstrated these agreements in the community that I lived in. I poured my heart into my children's school, my church, and my family. This consistently drained me, and recharging became difficult. I quickly started to understand that kindness and energy focused in the wrong direction was of no benefit to anyone. I was transformed, and the old me was no longer present. Attempting to bring change and awareness where it is not wanted is futile. Life experiences started pushing me out of my comfort zone. I no longer resonated with my old life. Vibrationally, I was not compatible with my surroundings, routine places, and people.

I fought this expansion for a few years, and it only got harder and more difficult to survive. Eventually, the universe took action and forced me to move through a series of events that drowned me out of the dream I had created. I had to eliminate the majority of people whom I no longer was in alignment with. Position, title, degree, blood relation became of no significance to me. Rude judgmental people fell off my radar. Inconsistent low-energy individuals repelled my existence, and false beliefs and teachings started falling away one by one. I discovered that family is people who choose you. Not people who tolerate you. Separating myself from the only world and people I had ever known became the hardest thing I had to do. It felt like death and separation from the known. I made the decision to love people in a different way. I walked away from people whom I loved deeply and still care for. My presence caused such discord that I felt it throughout my entire being. Transformation will often take you to places within yourself that are not pretty. Transformation is messy and scary at times. Surrender and allow it. Feel your way through. Source will guide you through the darkness and the unknown, and when you come out on the other side, brace yourself. Once you experience alignment with source that transforms every cell in your body, you can never return to the person you were before. That person no longer exists.

CHAPTER 13

THE POWER WITHIN

My desire to align daily so that I can impact those I love most is steadily gaining momentum. You must become selfish with your vibration until you understand and learn to effectively use the internal navigating system of emotions. Turn away from anything that feels bad or negative. Literally, look away from it; ignore it. Focus on good feelings, good thoughts, and good environments.

What is a good environment? A calm, quiet, peaceful environment as well as a fun, energetically flowing, and awe-inspiring environment. Flowing water fountains, fish aquariums, a fresh breeze, the smell of earth, the penetrating warmth of the sun, the presence of a faithful pet or the cool breeze felt under a shade tree. Music. Loud music. These are all examples of energetically charged environments for me. The connection that these types of environments allow and provide for me to connect with source is unequivocally valuable. I cannot buy enough merchandise, acquire enough fans or friends, create enough value, or work hard enough to become worthy of God's attention or favor. All that accomplishes is a resistance and block from the ever-present inheritance of just being me. Through alignment I gain a perspective and understanding that I am loved and favored and awarded God's favor and abundance without my action or effort. I am one of many branches of the creator. I am a source of universal knowledge and appreciation and blessings by my very existence and acknowledgment of who I am. I am an extension of all that is and ever has been. It is only in my cutting off, ignorance, and lack of understanding that I am not basking in the abundance that this material world has to offer. I am the creator of my life as well as receiver of the pleasure that I experience or desire to experience.

If I am not experiencing the energy and abundance offered to me, it is only because I am cutting off the flow with my internal self-talk and relationship with my source. My beliefs, opinions, and judgments of my experience and others constitutes my level of receptive ability between me and source. In reality, my relationship with source is all that matters. My ability to connect with and restore this relationship can be enhanced by my environment and the energies and influences that I allow in my presence. Whom I spend time with and what I choose to think about is either enhancing my alignment or cutting off my alignment with my inner source. To change any aspect of my life, I must become aware of the choices that I am making that prevent me from receiving and experiencing all the abundance and pleasure that are available to me. The power is within.

The choice is mine and mine alone. There is no "other" outside of my own internal dialogue that is preventing me from experiencing the life that I dream of. I am the creator of my experience, and I am the author and director of what is allowed to influence my choices and direction in life. As Voltaire said, "With great power comes great responsibility."

The more knowledge I acquire, the more alignment and connection I maintain with source, the more consciously aware I become of my need for this connection. Source is all I need. Source is all I desire to know and understand. Source is the secret, and alignment is the way. The choice to want a different life must first come with the understanding and acceptance that everything in our lives is a manifestation of our own internal commentary. Owning my own shit is a good place to start. Ownership. I am a child of God, and if I am not experiencing all that I desire to be and see and feel, then I must realize that I am the reason for the lack of what I desire. This understanding and ownership is the first step to creating and living the life we are meant to experience. Abundance is available for everyone to receive, and it is not based on our creative abilities, our hardworking ethics, our last name, or our association with anyone or anything. Creating the life we all desire is achievable by anyone of any culture, color, and nation. It is our birthright and inheritance from all that is. We are an extension of the source that creates worlds, and we have the ability to receive and become the supernatural beings that we truly are. Understanding and awareness will speed up the collective response that has already begun across the universe. Each individual has the opportunity to benefit from this knowledge. Some will not understand and will continue in their self-imposed bondage until they leave this present physical reality. Some will start to understand and will begin the process of alignment. This process is messy and challenging and at times scary. However, some will make a quantum leap with this knowledge and understanding. Some will resonate with this information and will feel the universal call of uniting love. Some will eliminate the resistance and beliefs that block the energetic flow of pure positive energy. All will experience this shift in positive and negatively perceived ways. All is necessary. Racism and prejudice will begin to dissipate. Divisions will burn out. We will ultimately unite and begin the expansion back to Eden and oneness.

CHAPTER 14

BECOMING A VIBRATIONAL SNOB: BRIDGING THE GAP

The collective consciousness is rising and shifting with or without our permission. Some of us are rising to the occasion with enough understanding that we desire to continue leading-edge evolution of asking, receiving, sifting, and sorting. As we sift through our daily life and experience, the wanted and unwanted, we are able to demonstrate the power of focus through consistent, daily alignment. Creating our outer world is as easy as shifting our focus through daily alignment within our inner world. You must become selfish with your time and attention. Alignment will allow you to connect with source, where inspiration and fun-fueled action will follow. The gap between where you currently are vibrationally and where your inner source resides is simply an awareness. An awareness coupled with an understanding of the accumulation of all your cooperative components and the realization that this human experience has been gifted with an internal navigating system capable of complete alignment with source. Everything is in your favor. Place your focus on the desired feeling that you wish to experience and the cooperative components will show up at the right place and at the right time. Take your eyes and attention off of anything and anyone that interferes with your good feeling vibration until you achieve a desired emotional set point that is unaffected by your environment. Our beliefs and mindset give rise to the idea that there is a gap between where we are and where we want to be. This is a false belief because what we are seeking is a feeling not a place. The feeling can be achieved in the now.

To understand this gap, let me tell you about Titus. Titus was an upper-seventies-year-old patient of mine a few years back. He suffered daily from end-stage COPD (chronic obstructive pulmonary disorder). Titus gave me a beautiful perspective of what it was like to be in a situation of physical and emotional suffering and desire to not be there.

One day we had a very intense conversation that I will never forget. Typically I ask my patients what their future goals include. On this day, Titus was feeling about the same as always, which was tired, short of breath, fatigued, and discouraged. "I want to be able to walk outside to the edge of my yard and back to the house without getting short of breath," proclaimed Titus. This seems like a reasonable goal for most but not for Titus, and we both knew it. I asked him if he was interested in physical therapy, and he responded, "Yes." I think we both knew this was not going to be effective at this point either, but I always wanted to be positive and supportive so I agreed.

At the end of my visit, I sat down at the kitchen table with Titus and asked him, "What is your biggest fear right now?" Titus looked up at me like he had been waiting months for someone to ask him that very question and said, "If my house was to catch on fire, I could not physically get my family out safely." We both sat in that silence for a long time, and he then said, "I feel so powerless and weak. I don't want to feel this way anymore." I heard what he was saying, but I also felt what he was feeling. Powerlessness to do and be what he needed to be. I also knew that he was living in the past, and I wanted to help him overcome this terrible reality he was living in his mind.

I thought about it for a minute, and then I said, "You are suffering from something that is not necessary." He looked at me very suspiciously but said, "Go on."

"Clearly you understand your physical limitations, and they are causing you a great deal of suffering and poor quality of life." He nodded in agreement. "But here's the thing: nobody needs you to help them get out of a house fire, even if you did have one. Your family is all grown up. Your wife is healthy, and your adult son is helping you most of the time. You are looking at your expectations from a flawed perspective, which is causing a gap from where you are at to where you want to be."

His wife walked over to the table and said, "Honey, I can get my own self out of the house, and I love you no matter how fast or far you can walk." His son looked up from across the room and said, "Dad, we can all get out together. We are a team, and nobody is responsible for everyone here." All three of them were serious and looking directly at each other.

I felt the room get warm, and I relaxed and leaned back in my chair with a smile stretching across my face. "You don't need to change a thing to feel good right now. Everything that is important to you is here with you."

At that moment he realized that he had been suffering and living with daily regret over something that was not even happening or truth to anyone but himself. It was all in his mind. Fear, the past, undesired future events, weaknesses, failures … all were unwanted thoughts and events that created unwanted feelings and emotions that were keeping him from living the life that was right in front of him. In fact, this gentleman had been living the majority of his life with thoughts about future and past events that had never happened anywhere but in his own mind.

Titus lived the remainder of his days with a slightly different perspective every time I came to see him. Over the next month, I saw and felt a beautiful transformation that we all felt during that visit when Titus just let go of the irrational delusion that he needed to be someone he wasn't, with abilities that he did not need. The gap of suffering dissolved. It was no longer an obstacle to feel and rehearse in his mind.

Our relationship with source is the same exact way. Most people suffer and strive every day toward a goal or a feeling that is available right now. The gap from where we are currently to where we want to be is imaginary. Of course, I understand that if you desire a yacht and you do not have one, then you cannot make it magically appear just by thinking you already have it. However, it is only the thought of not having it that causes the discord and lack of contentment. You can be content and happy and joyful on your way to attaining the yacht. It all starts in the now. Changing our perspective and getting aligned with source will bring the satisfaction and contentment that we all seek. In that knowing and alignment, everything that we desire begins to manifest into our reality. Once you begin to cultivate this beautiful alignment on a consistent basis, the momentum will build, and joy will be the dominant vibration. Joy, freedom, love, and empowerment are the results of alignment with source. As Ram Dass said, "We are all just walking each other home."

The Vibrational Knob

EPILOGUE

The highest vibration is love. Love is the answer. Love is powerful and when properly understood and used it is transformational. As we continue to expand and grow, the heart of source will become more evident in each individuals lives. My challenge is that each person reading this book will tune into their inner GPS system through alignment. Meditation, appreciation and contemplation will align your heart with your inner source and guide you through inspired action.

My fascination, love and admiration for the masculine species has broken my heart on more than one occasion but fixed my vision. May all who accept my challenge for alignment start with a commitment to speak truth from the heart. The heart is the strongest force on this planet and we must be brave enough to protect it and use it for our own expansion and growth. The heart will guide the steps of those that seek its direction. Tolerating lies and excuses will weaken the hearts impulse causing resistance within the internal

GPS system. The spoken word has power. A power that the heart and mind understand and respond to.

My Love Letter to the Universe.

May I speak with love as a powerful creator to all that will receive my words. I find no greater force in the world more powerful than the spoken word fueled by truth and love. I bow my head in submission to the source within and desire the divine virtues of courage, wisdom, justice, temperance and compassion to invade my being. May these virtues flow through my words to all my feminine and masculine counterparts as the collective vibration rises and the heart of source, compassion, overcomes all resistance.

REFERENCES

Abraham et al. *Ask And It Is Given: Learning To Manifest Your Desires.* Hay House, 2009.

Dass, Ram. *Walking Each Other Home: Conversations on Love and Dying.* Sounds True, 2018.

Dispenza, Joe and Gregg Braden. *Becoming Supernatural: How Common People*

Are Doing The Uncommon. Hay House Inc, 2019.

Http://www.goalcast.com/2017/12/20/25nikola-tesla-quotes

Http://www.biograghy.com/people/alberteinstein-9285408.

Https://www.brainyquote.com/quotes/josephcampbell-134756.

Printed in the United States
By Bookmasters